CELLS

THE BUILDING BLOCKS OF LIFE

Plant Cells

Cells: The Building Blocks of Life

CELLS

THE BUILDING BLOCKS OF LIFE

Plant Cells

BRAD FITZPATRICK

CHELSEA HOUSE
An Infobase Learning Company

PLANT CELLS

Copyright © 2011 by Infobase Learning

Chelsea House
An imprint of Infobase Learning
132 West 31st Street
New York NY 10001

Library of Congress Cataloging-in-Publication Data

Fitzpatrick, Brad.
Plant cells / Brad Fitzpatrick.
    p. cm. — (Cells: the building blocks of life)
 Includes bibliographical references and index.
 ISBN 978-1-61753-009-8 (hardcover)
 1. Plant cells and tissues. I. Title. II. Series: Cells: the building blocks of life.
 QK725.F58 2011
 571.6'3829—dc22   2011006947

Text design and composition by Erika K. Arroyo
Cover design by Alicia Post
Cover printed by Yurchak Printing, Landisville, Pa.
Book printed and bound by Yurchak Printing, Landisville, Pa.
Date printed: September 2011
Printed in the United States of America

10 9 8 7 6 5 4 3 2 1

This book is printed on acid-free paper.

All links and Web addresses were checked and verified to be correct at the time of publication. Because of the dynamic nature of the Web, some addresses and links may have changed since publication and may no longer be valid.

On the cover: A cross-section of collenchyma tissue from a stem

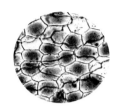

Contents

● ● ●

Introduction to the Cell

Englishman Robert Hooke was one of the most brilliant scientists of the seventeenth century. He worked as an architect, mathematician, and scientist and added greatly to the knowledge of scientific principles of his day. Hooke made his best-known discovery in 1665 while he was a member of the Royal Society of Scientists. King Charles II asked Hooke to examine insects using a new invention called the microscope, the first of which had been developed less than 100 years before in the Netherlands by an eyeglass maker who used glass lenses to enable the viewing of objects in close up and in greater detail. Hooke did as the king asked and, with his rudimentary microscope (which was made out of leather and gold), he launched his investigation of the components that make up living things.

Although he was only asked to study insects, Hooke went further. His amazement with what he saw through the lens of his microscope soon led him to examine a variety of other materials and organisms. Hooke became so fascinated that he even allowed lice to suck the blood from his hand so he could watch how the blood flowed through the insects' body.

Hooke's best known discovery using the microscope came when he examined a piece of cut cork. He saw that the cork was made up of a series of small chambers, or openings. Hooke was puzzled by these small pores, which he called "cells" from the Latin *celle*, meaning "chamber." Hooke immediately recognized that these small cells were significant, even though he did not know exactly what they were. Hooke wrote, "Now, though I have with great diligence [tried] to find whether there be any

FIGURE 1.1 British scientist Robert Hooke made numerous discoveries in fields as diverse as astronomy and microbiology, yet there are no portraits of him. Thus, this bust—from the Hooke Museum on the Isle of Wight in the United Kingdom—was based only on written descriptions of him. While there is some controversy over why this is the case, some historians suggest that fellow British scientist Isaac Newton, who died 24 years later, attempted to eradicate Hooke's likeness from history due to their long rivalry over studies in light and gravitation, amongst other things.

such thing in those microscopical pores of wood or piths, as the valves in the heart, veins and other passages of animals, that open and give passage to the contained fluid juices one way, and shut themselves, and impede the passage of such [liquids] back."

Hooke did not know exactly what he discovered, but he went on to compare cells in cork, which comes from the inner portion of the cork tree, to other types of plant tissues like leaves and roots. His works, which were the first writings about what is now called **cell theory**, were published in 1665 in his book *Micrographia: Or Some Physiological Descriptions Of Minute Bodies Made By Magnifying Glasses: With Observations And Inquiries Thereupon.* Cell theory states that all living things are made of cells, that cells reproduce to make more cells, and that cells form the basic building blocks for all living things. Hooke was the first to understand that cells were the building blocks of life and is often credited as the father of cell theory. While Hooke's discovery of cells make him one of the world's most famous biologists, he considered himself to be a mathematician and physicist. He admitted that he did not completely understand how cells worked, but he believed that cells were the holding containers for what he labeled the "noble juices"—fluids within the plant that made it a living thing. He tried to attribute the principles of physics to the energy within cells, trying to explain that energy traveled through cells in waves. Hooke died in 1703 without ever fully understanding the discovery he had made that day in 1665.

Hooke truly believed he had found something of scientific importance when he looked at the cork, and he was correct. His was the first clear description of how the living tissue of plants was made of small, regular chambers he called cells. However, although Hooke knew that cells were the building block of plant tissues, it was not until after his death that scientists truly began to understand that all living things are made up of cells and that these cells undergo the processes of life.

It wasn't until almost 200 years later that German botanist Matthias Jakob Schleiden began to describe the principles of cell theory as they pertained to living things, particularly plants. German zoologist Theodor Schwann, a contemporary of Schleiden's, further elaborated on his findings by saying that animals, like plants, were comprised entirely of cells and that new cells came from preexisting cells. Another German scientist, Rudolf Virchow, began applying the principles of cell theory to medicine in the mid-nineteenth century. The findings of Hooke and, later, Schleiden, Schwann, and Virchow gave rise to a new era in scientific discovery as sci-

ANCIENT DESERT PLANT

Welwitschia mirabilis is one of the world's most ancient and least-understood species of plants. This plant, which lives only in the deserts of southwestern Africa, resembles strands of thick green ribbon that unfurl from a central single stem. Individual *Welwitschia* plants can live to be hundreds of years old as they spread their green, leathery leaves across the dry desert ground. The center of each plant contains a woody disk that grows in diameter as the plant ages. A single, sturdy taproot runs deep into the sandy desert soil to keep the plant from being pulled out of the ground.

One of the most unique characteristics of *Welwitschia* is its ability to survive in some of the world's driest and most desolate landscapes, such as Namibia's Namib Desert, an area that is almost totally devoid of water for most of the year. The thick green leaves of this plant look odd in the otherwise grey, rocky, barren Namib. *Welwitschia* plants are able to survive in such extreme conditions because the plant has adapted a unique method for collecting water. Each morning, dense fog banks hang over the Namib Desert, the result of moisture driven inland by coastal winds from the Atlantic Ocean. This fog settles and briefly forms a thin, shimmering coat of dew over the desert that evaporates soon after the desert Sun rises. During the brief period of time when dew is on the ground, the *Welwitschia* collects the moisture that settles on its leaves, thanks to its **stomata**, or small pores, that are found on both sides of the leaves. (Most plants have stomata only on the underside of their leaves.) As soon as the dew begins to evaporate, the stomata close

entists began to examine cells more closely in order to understand what occurred on a microscopic level within the boundaries of the small boxes that Hooke had discovered with his crude microscope.

Today, scientists know that all living things—from the giant coniferous trees of the western United States to microscopic organisms floating in the ocean—are made up of one or more cells. Although Hooke thought that cells existed simply to move materials from one area to another, scientists have since discovered that cells carry out a wide variety of tasks

up to hold in any moisture that the plant has collected from the dew. Despite efforts to grow *Welwitschia* domestically, this ancient plant has proven almost impossible to cultivate because of the highly specialized environment it is adapted to.

Figure 1.2 *Welwitschia mirabilis* blooms is in Namib Desert, which stretches through Namibia and Angola, Africa.

that are required for life. Cells transport materials, make energy, remove wastes, reproduce, respond to outside stimuli, and defend themselves. Some cells, such as single-celled algal plants that live in the water, can even move when necessary. Cells come in a variety of shapes and sizes to perform a variety of tasks. The delicate pink petals of a rose, the thorny skin of a cactus, and the green leaves of a summer tree are all made of cells that help that plant perform the necessary tasks to survive. Like all living things, cells are born and eventually die.

MODERN CELL THEORY

Scientists who study the nature of cells are commonly called cell biologists. **Biology** is the study of living things, from single-celled, microscopic organisms to the largest, most complex organisms on Earth.

Early cell biologists set out to study the processes that a cell goes through as it is created, undergoes the processes of life, and dies. These cell biologists, intrigued by Robert Hooke's discovery in 1665, continued studying plant and animal cells and quickly realized that, although both

SUPER SEAWEED: IS KELP A PLANT?

Kelp, which grows in shallow, cold ocean waters, is often referred to as seaweed. You may wonder, how does a plant, which requires light for photosynthesis, survive while living at the bottom of the ocean? Kelp, despite its weedy appearance, is actually not a plant at all. Kelp is created by specialized algae that form "forests" in cold coastal waters around the world. Some of the largest kelp forests in the United States can be found off the coast of California where seals, sharks, and other marine animals rely on the kelp forests to provide them with shelter and nutrients.

It is easy to understand why kelp could be confused with plants. Kelp forms what appear to be leaves as well as roots that anchor it into the ocean floor. Kelp grows extremely quickly, sometimes as much a foot a day, in its effort to reach the sunlight near the ocean's surface. Why? Because like plants, kelp rely on sunlight for food. The algae that form the great forests of kelp actually use the same process that plants use to create food, transferring energy from sunlight into nutrients that the plant requires for cell growth.

Kelp is harvested for a variety of uses. It is very high in nutrients and vitamins, and many people eat kelp or take it in pill form as a dietary supplement. Kelp may also provide a clean, renewable energy source. It breaks down very quickly and produces methane gas. This gas, in turn, could be used to provide energy and heat. However, kelp forests, despite their ability to regenerate rapidly, are susceptible to damage by humans. Global warming is one of the biggest threats facing kelp forests since these forests can only survive in cold water. As the world's oceans warm, available habitat for kelp disappears.

types of cells carried out the necessary life processes, plant and animal cells were also very different in a variety of ways. For instance, scientists began to investigate how plants could make their own food from sunlight when other organisms like humans had to consume other living things. Scientists also wondered why the outside portion of plant cells was thicker and more geometrically regular than the cells of animals.

Today, scientists know a great deal about plant cells. They understand the complex and unique systems that take place inside the cells of plants

Figure 1.3 Kelp forests grow quickly underwater in shallow oceans.

that allow simple seeds on the forest floor to grow into massive trees. One of the greatest mysteries of plant survival, the ability to produce food, was solved when scientists looked into the heart of the plant cell. In fact, all of the processes required of a living organism lie hidden within a single plant cell.

Modern technology has also allowed scientists to manipulate plants. By understanding the nature of the plant cell, scientists have been able to modify plants for human uses. Plants provide us with clothing, medicine, food, and building materials. Humans could not survive without the plants that grow all around us. Each year, more species of plants are discovered, and some of them may hold the secrets to curing serious illnesses, such as cancer. Today, there are more than 260,000 known species of plants and each year that number increases as scientists around the world identify brand new species. Plants play a vital role in our lives. And plants, no matter how large or small, all have one thing in common—all of them are made of plant cells.

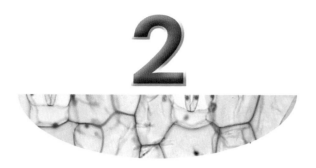

2

Parts of
the Plant Cell

Both plants and animals are made of cells. Plants and animals share many similar characteristics and many of the same organelles. An **organelle** is a specialized unit within the cell that performs a specific function. Organelles act in much the same way our heart, liver, and lungs do. Each organ in our body has a specific function that it carries out that helps us survive. Organelles act in the same way. Some of the organelles that both plant and animal cells share include nuclei, ribosomes, and golgi bodies.

There are, however, major differences between plant and animal cells in both their structure and their organelles. The three main differences are cell walls, vacuoles, and chloroplasts.

CELL WALL

When Robert Hooke first examined the cells in that piece of cork in 1665, he saw empty cavities within a matrix of fibrous material. What Hooke was actually looking at were the remains of thousands of cell walls. All of the organelles of each cell, including the nucleus and the cytoplasm, had dried up. However, the cell walls remained. These remaining cell walls actually kept many scientists from accepting the cell theory immediately. Animal tissue has no such walls, so many scientists believed that the matrix that Hooke called cells only existed in plants. Eventually, though, advances in microscopy and further research showed that both plants and animals were made of cells.

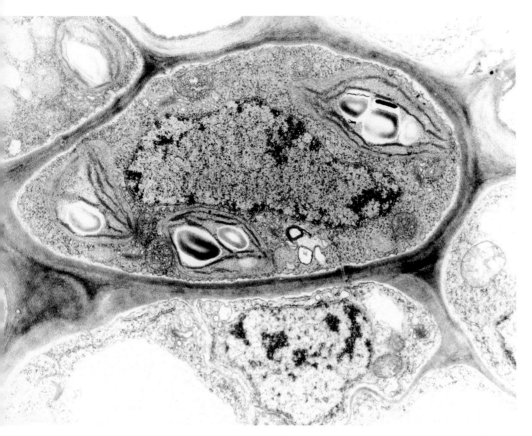

FIGURE 2.1 In this transmission electron microscope image, a plant cell, from a weed called *Chenopodium album*, is shown. The nucleus is orange, the chloroplasts are dark green, and the mitochondrion is red.

A plant's **cell wall** surrounds the plant cell and provides protection and support for the interior portion of the cell. The cell wall begins developing when the plant is still in its earliest stages of development. Early in the life of a plant, the cell walls are thinner and more flexible to allow for rapid growth.

Despite the fact that cell walls appear rigid, they are actually made mostly of water. Cellulose, a type of polysaccharide carbohydrate, makes up a great deal of the cell wall. The cellulose in plant cell walls is formed when long chains of the sugar glucose are bonded by hydrogen atoms. The structure of cellulose is very similar to that of starch, which is a common ingredient in foods that we eat. Cellulose, which differs from starch only by the location of certain bonds, is impossible for animals to break down. In fact, even a termite, which feeds off the wood pulp, cannot break down and digest the wood it eats without the aid of bacteria that live inside its digestive system. Because animals, including humans, cannot break down the cellulose in plants, it passes through the digestive system without being absorbed. Diets that are high in cellulose, which is oftentimes referred to as fiber, help maintain digestive health.

The cell wall serves the plant in a variety of ways. First, as we discussed earlier, plant cell walls provide plant cells with a solid structure that helps protect the interior portion of the cell. This strong framework also allows many plant cells to be placed on top of one another without damaging other cells. This is not the case with animal cell walls. For example, the human body could not bear our weight if we were 50 feet tall (15.2 meters), yet many tree species grow even larger than that without running the risk of crushing themselves. This strong framework of cell walls also makes wood and other materials useful because they can withstand a great amount of pressure without breaking. Your desk at school, the chair you sit at and the dining room table you eat on and even the boards that form the framework of your home are all strengthened by individual cell walls and the carbohydrate complex called cellulose that cell walls are made of.

Cell walls also protect the plant in other ways, as well. For instance, without the cell wall, large particles or toxic substances might be able to reach the cell's interior. Plant cells create what is called a physical barrier, a wall that keeps unwanted materials from entering and damaging the cell.

Another function of the cell wall is to maintain a condition known as osmotic balance. Understanding the processes of diffusion and osmosis is essential to appreciating what a cell must do to maintain its size, structure, and chemical balance. Diffusion is the natural tendency for molecules to spread out inside of a medium like air or water. Whether you know it or not, you are already familiar with the process of diffusion. Have you ever opened your refrigerator and shuddered at the smell of spoiled food? Have you ever smelled the scent of your favorite food cooking on the stove? If so, then you have experienced diffusion. The good or bad smells that you experienced were due to the fact that molecules from the food spread out into the air and reached your nose.

Osmosis is similar to diffusion in many ways. For starters, osmosis and diffusion both occur because molecules naturally tend to spread out. Sometimes, however, molecules want to spread out but are blocked by a barrier of some kind. Sometimes water is able to cross through a membrane to reach this group of molecules. The more water that gets through, the more these molecules can spread out. Because of osmosis, cells will either swell or shrink depending upon the nature of the solution they are located in. For instance, a cell that has more salt molecules inside it than there are in the surrounding water is said to be in a **hypotonic solution** because there is less salt in the solution (water) around the cell. Because there is a high concentration of salt inside the cell, water from the outside of the cell will rush in and cause the cell to increase in size. A cell that contains less salt than the surrounding water is said to be in a **hypertonic solution**. In this case, there is more salt in the water surrounding the cell than there is in the water inside the cell. Being in a hypertonic solution causes cells to decrease the amount of water that is inside them.

Cells that do not have a cell wall are at risk of **cellular lysis**. This is a process in which a cell pulls in so much water through osmosis that it actually bursts and dies. Plant cells, with their rigid cell walls, are protected from going through cellular lysis.

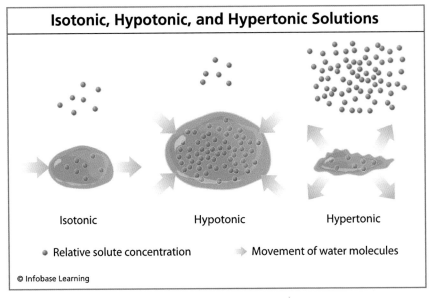

FIGURE 2.2 This illustration shows the effects of different salt solutions on living cells. Isotonic solutions have the same salt concentration as the cell interior, so the cells retain their normal size and shape. Cells placed in a hypotonic solution gain water and swell because the concentration of solutes in hypotonic solutions is less than in cells, which generates a driving force for water to flow into cells by osmosis. In contrast, cells placed in hypertonic solutions tend to shrink from loss of water.

Plant cell walls are not completely rigid, however. They can bend and stretch without breaking, thanks to the water that is stored within the cell wall. You can see this effect when you try to pull a plant stem apart. The tensile ability of the cell walls allows the plant to stretch before breaking. Certain plants like seaweed must be able to bend. Otherwise, the strong ocean current would break them apart.

The cell wall is not completely solid, though. It is essential for plant cells to be able to pass materials in and out of the cell. The cell wall, therefore, has a series of pores that allow materials to pass in and out as needed. When food and water are brought into the cell, the waste materials created as byproducts of photosynthesis are allowed to pass out of the cell wall. This is due to the microscopic pores lining the wall that allow the waste materials to flow in and out. These pores in the cell wall will also change their size, depending upon the conditions surrounding the cell. This flexibility helps the cell control the amount of materials flowing in and out. In times of drought, for instance, pores in the cell wall may shrink to keep water in and avoid dehydration. This ability to control the flow of materials through the cell wall is one of the most important adaptations for plant survival.

Even though plant cell walls are extremely thin, they have a high level of tensile strength. Tensile strength is the ability of a material to resist breaking when stretched. The bonds in plant cell walls form a network that resists being broken. If you've ever tried to pull a weed from your yard, you will see that despite their thin stems, plants have an amazing ability to resist breaking. This is due to the strength of the bonds within the matrix that makes up the cell wall. The cell walls in plants actually have a higher level of tensile strength than steel.

If plant cells were completely rigid, then plants would not be able to grow. Plant cell walls, therefore, must be able to change their composition when needed. Hormonal changes in the plant cell allow it to be solid when working to support the plant (like the tree trunk that must support the tree's tremendous weight) or soft during periods of growth and expansion.

If cell walls were truly solid, then it would be impossible for plants to pass materials from one cell to another. Therefore, small passageways exist between the plant cell walls to move materials from one cell to the next. These small channels are called **plasmodesmata.** Since plant cells work independently to support the entire organism, it is essential that plants be able to easily send food, water, and hormones from one cell to the next. Eduard Tangel, a scientist who studied the structure of cell walls in the

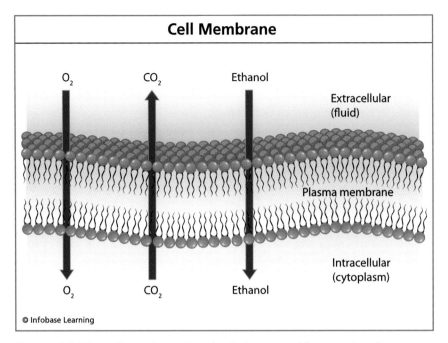

Cell Membrane

O_2 CO_2 Ethanol

Extracellular (fluid)

Plasma membrane

Intracellular (cytoplasm)

O_2 CO_2 Ethanol

© Infobase Learning

FIGURE 2.3 The cell membrane is selectively permeable, meaning that some substances can pass through it and some cannot. Fat-soluble substances, such as oxygen, carbon dioxide, and alcohol, pass through cell membranes by simple diffusion because they can dissolve in the lipid bilayer.

late nineteenth century, discovered that dyes introduced into one plant cell could pass to other cells. This indicated that cells had the ability to move materials from one to the next as needed. Each plant cell actually has several of these openings so that large amounts of materials can pass from one plant cell to the next.

In the area between the cell wall and the cell interior is the **cell membrane**. Also known as a plasma membrane, this acts to separate the interior portion of the cell from the external environment. The cell membrane lies just inside the cell wall and is less rigid. The cell membrane does not contain the same cellulose that makes up the cell wall around it. Cell walls are one difference between plant and animal cells, but cell membranes are found in both types of cells. Like the cell wall, the cell membrane protects the interior of the cell by determining which materials can pass in and out.

Cell walls are highly specialized and allow plants to live in a variety of locations and undergo many life processes.

TEAMWORK BETWEEN TREES AND ANTS

Acacia trees, which are covered with long, sharply pointed thorns, seem like a formidable plant that would have few natural enemies. However, these trees, which are native to South America and Africa, are at risk from herbivores that eat their leaves and insects that damage both the leaves and stems.

Acacia trees have developed a unique system of protection that involves organisms thousands of times smaller than the tree itself. Acacia trees produce a sweet, sappy nectar that they release through several locations on the tree called nectaries. These nectaries draw ants to come and feed on this free meal provided by the tree. In addition, the acacia's massive thorns are hollow, which allows the ants to use them as nests.

In return for the food and shelter provided by the tree, ants fiercely defend their home and food source. They will actually attack and kill other insects that land on the tree and keep them from harming the acacia. Even large herbivores like deer and gazelles are not safe from the hordes of ants that stand guard over the tree. In fact, the ants will attack anything that tries to feed off their acacia home. This type of relationship is known as a symbiotic relationship, meaning that both the tree and the ants benefit from this partnership. The ants are provided with a home and a food source by the tree, while the tree is protected by the thousands of ants that call it home.

Figure 2.4 Stinging *Pseudomyrmex spinicola* ants gather food on an Acacia tree.

VACUOLES

When you look at a plant cell under a light microscope, a large portion of the plant cell appears to be empty. Why is this so, and what purpose does this large, seemingly vacant space serve?

Early cell biologists asked that same question. Lazzaro Spallanzani, an eighteenth-century Italian scientist, first observed these empty spaces in the cells of protozoa, which are simple, single-celled organisms. Spallanzani was baffled by these empty spaces, which he believed had something to do with respiration. Scientist Félix Dujardin, another plant biologist who was puzzled by these empty areas, called these spaces *vacuoles*, after the Latin word for "empty."

Vacuoles, however, are not really made up of empty space. A vacuole is an organelle within the cell that is surrounded by a membrane and contains a liquid solution of water and other materials such as enzymes. They serve to maintain osmotic balance in the plant cell by increasing and decreasing their volume according to the conditions in and around the cell. They can be found in some animal cells, but they are much larger in plant cells. Vacuoles have no definite shape and can increase or decrease in size depending upon conditions. Under a microscope, vacuoles often appear as large openings in the cell that typically comprise about a quarter of the interior of the cell. Vacuoles can expand depending on the osmotic conditions and may take up as much as 80% of the total cell.

Vacuoles play a variety of roles in the plant cell. One of their most important roles is in the control and removal of toxic substances. Plant cells are vulnerable to toxins created as a byproduct of normal cellular activity. There are also toxins in the environment like pollutants that can kill plant cells. These toxins must be separated within the cell so that they do not damage other organelles until they can be broken down by enzymes and returned to the cytoplasm within the cell. Vacuoles store toxins until they can be broken down and removed from the cell. This is also why certain plants, such as tomatoes (which are often grown in very salty soil), do not produce fruit that has an elevated salt content. This is because when the salt from the soil enters the plant, it is stored in vacuoles in the leaves.

Another way in which vacuoles help protect the plant cell is by balancing the pH within the cell. **pH** is the measure of how acidic or basic a substance is. For plants to survive, pH levels must remain constant. The inside of a vacuole has a low pH and is, therefore, a base. Because of this, ions (which are elements with a positive or negative charge) within the cell can be moved in or out of the vacuole easily.

Perhaps the most important function of the vacuole is in maintaining turgor pressure within the cell. Turgor pressure in plant cells is the amount of pressure that the vacuole exerts on the cell walls. When water is abundant, vacuoles will fill and take up a great deal of the space within the plant cell, increasing turgor pressure and causing the plant cell to swell. The vacuole can expand and contract in size and acts much like a balloon that is filled with water. This helps to keep the plant rigid and upright. When water is scarce, however, vacuoles will shrink due to the lack of water within their membrane. The result is lower turgor pressure on the cell walls. The plant will lose its rigidity and begin to wilt or droop. Vacuoles also help plants gather food by allowing leaves and branches to spread out and remain rigid, which allows for more sunlight to be absorbed. This increases the plant's ability to make food.

Inside the plant cell, vacuoles oftentimes separate molecules that will react with one another if they come in contact. For instance, slicing onions produces a gas that irritates the eyes and nose. This gas forms when the vacuoles of an onion cell are cut open. This allows molecules to blend together to form propanethiol S-oxide, the chemical cocktail responsible for the irritating odor produced by cutting onions.

Vacuoles are not limited to plant cells. Fungi, animal, and bacterial cells all have vacuoles, as well. However, the size and multitude of functions that the vacuole serves in plant cells differs greatly from those in animal and bacterial cells. In animal cells, for instance, vacuoles are much smaller and serve mainly to help the cell reduce and control wastes.

CHLOROPLASTS

Plants are essential to life on Earth because of their unique ability to make food from the Sun's radiant energy through a process known as photosynthesis. For this reason, plants are classified in a group of organisms called **autotrophs**. An autotroph can produce food energy from nonliving sources. The word *autotroph* comes from the Latin term that means "self feeding." This ability to harness energy from sunlight allows for all life on Earth to exist.

One of the unique components of plant cells that sets them apart from animal cells is the presence of **chloroplasts**. Chloroplasts are the organelles that allow the plant to take energy from sunlight and convert it into nourishing sugars. They are shaped like disks and are usually green due to the presence of **chlorophyll**, a pigment that gives most living plant cells their color.

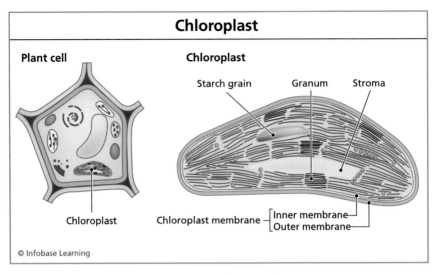

Chloroplast

Plant cell

Chloroplast

Starch grain   Granum   Stroma

Chloroplast

Chloroplast membrane — ⎡Inner membrane⎤
⎣Outer membrane⎦

© Infobase Learning

FIGURE 2.5 A chloroplast is the site of photosynthesis in a plant cell.

There are many theories as to the origin of chloroplasts in plant cells. The most common theory states that chloroplasts are actually derived from symbiotic bacteria called cyanobacteria. Nineteenth-century Russian scientist Konstantin Mereschkowski believed that plants develop the ability to undergo photosynthesis when they join with bacteria capable of turning radiant energy into food. Mereschkowski called this process, in which two organisms living in symbiosis form a single organism, **endosymbiosis**. Today, many scientists believe that the chloroplasts in plants may be the product of endosymbiosis between primitive plants and bacteria.

As early as the 1600s, botanists were intrigued by the green material that gave plants their color. Advances in microscopy allowed scientists in the early 1800s to examine the green material in plants more closely. They found that this green pigment was housed in small disks. Although most of these disks were elliptical in shape, others came in a variety of different shapes. However, these early scientists also found that even in a green leaf, not all of these disks, which were first called chlorophyll granules, were green. A few of them were a yellow-orange color. Others appeared to have no color at all.

This discovery fascinated scientists of the period. Chief among them was plant biologist Karl Friedric Schimper, who studied plant cells in Germany in the 1800s. In 1883, while examining the many green, yellow, and clear chlorophyll granules in a plant cell, Schimper decided to classify each color separately. The clear ones he called leucoplasts. The yellow ones were dubbed chromoplasts.

Chloroplasts make up the bulk of the plastid content in plant cells. Usually oblong or oval shaped, chloroplasts are surrounded by a double layer of membranes that separate them from the cytoplasm of the cell. Inside the membrane, the components of the chloroplast float in a fluid material known as stroma.

Inside the chloroplast, supported and surrounded by the stroma, are groups of stacked membranes that resemble stacks of pancakes. These groups of membranes are usually green in color and called **grana**. Each individual granum (singular of grana) is itself a series of thin membranes that are called **thylakoids**, which are stacked one atop the other. Thylakoids are where those reactions that turn radiant light energy into food take place, the process known as photosynthesis.

Plants do not turn green unless they are exposed to sunlight. This is because chloroplasts (which develop from cells known as proplastids) will not develop the pigments necessary for turning light energy into food if no light is initially present. When you look at portions of plants growing under objects such as old tires or a piece of wood and away from sunlight, you will see that those portions will be white and not green. Likewise, plant roots will not turn green because photosynthesis cannot occur in areas of the plant where light cannot reach.

Other structures in plant cells further distinguish them from animal cells. Plant cells are unique because of their ability to produce energy from **inorganic materials**, which are materials that come from nonliving sources. The inorganic material that plants use to produce energy is the radiant energy produced by the Sun. However, plant and animal cells are similar in some ways, as you will read in the next chapters. Ultimately all cells, whether plant or animal cells, share a common goal—to carry out the processes of life.

NUCLEUS: MASTER OF THE CELL

One essential organelle in all cells is the **nucleus**. A cell's nucleus contains nucleic acids that provide the blueprints for the production of proteins and the expression of **genes**. Genes are the hereditary units of living organisms and they determine how an organism grows, carries out life functions, and finally dies. Genes that are present at our birth determine how tall we will be, what color eyes and hair we will have, and whether or not we will have certain diseases. Just as in humans, genes in the nucleus control the life of plants.

The very first scientist to recognize that the nucleus was a unique portion of the cell was Antonie van Leeuwenhoek, who first sketched nuclei for the Royal Society of London, an exclusive group of England's premier scientists, in the early 1700s. Even though van Leeuwenhoek was the first to recognize that the nucleus was a separate portion of the cell, it was Scottish botanist Robert Brown who first described the nature of the nucleus in 1831. Brown was studying the reproductive cycles of plants and spent a great deal of time examining plant cells under a microscope. During the course of his studies, Brown noticed that each of the cells he looked at had a similar formation near the center of the cell. Brown did not immediately recognize the significance of what he was looking at. He wrote that he found a "single circular areola, generally somewhat less opaque than the membrane of the cell." He also wrote that "this areola, which is more or less distinctly granular, is slightly convex, and although it seems to be on the surface is in reality covered by the outer lamina of the cell."

Brown briefly described this "circular areola," which he called a nucleus after the Latin word for a seed or kernel. Even so, Brown gave little thought to the importance of the nucleus. Later, the German botanist Matthias Jakob Schleiden came to believe that the nucleus, or "cytoblast," as he called it, played a vital role in the life cycle of the plant. He correctly hypothesized that the nucleus was an important element in cell reproduction. Schleiden reviewed Brown's work and began to study the nucleus and its role in the growth of plants and formation of new cells. Schleiden and fellow German scientist Theodor Schwann began to compare their findings in the late 1830s. Schwann, who was a zoologist, noticed that animal cells also had a nucleus. Together, the scientists concluded that the nucleus of a cell is responsible for organizing the cell's reproductive process. Schwann, Schleiden, and Rudolf Virchow developed the first true cell theory based upon Robert Hooke's 1665 discovery of cells and the subsequent scientific data that pointed to them as the repeating unit that makes up living things.

Despite Schleiden's keen observations about the cell and the role of the nucleus, he did not completely understand how nuclei work and how they originated. As a matter of fact, Schleiden wasn't sure that all the cells he examined even had nuclei because during certain periods in the cell's life, the nucleus is difficult to observe. Eventually, the development of stains and dyes for use in microscopic work in the late 1800s led Eduard

Zacharias, a German cell biologist, to conclude in 1881 that the nucleus of a cell, which is easily revealed by staining, contained materials that served some important purpose. He called these easily dyed internal parts of the nucleus *chromatin*, which literally means "colored material" in Latin. Inside the chromatin, he noted a mass of material that was later named **chromosomes**, from the Latin for "colored bodies."

Up until this point, scientists had located and named some of the various parts of the nucleus, but they had not fully begun to understand the processes that these materials undergo during the period of the cell's life. In the mid-1880s German botanist Hugo de Vries (1848-1935) began to describe the role of the nucleus in the reproduction of cells. De Vries also was the first to discern the fact that the chromosomes in the nucleus play a vital role in **heredity**. *Heredity* refers to the passing down of traits from a parent to its offspring.

Today, we know that the nucleus of a cell, be it a plant cell or animal cell, is responsible for the control of the expression of genes that are coded for in our **DNA**. DNA, or **deoxyribonucleic acid**, contains essential genetic information. The cell's DNA is a warehouse that contains all of the essential information about that cell.

DNA is made up of long chains of polymers that are made of materials called nucleotides. Nucleotides contain sugars and bases and form the backbone of the long, twisted double helix shape that we associate with DNA. DNA contain four bases—adenine, guanine, cytosine, and thymine. These bases form bonds with a specific type of base on the corresponding strand of DNA in the double helix. Adenine bases bond to thymine bases, and cytosine bases bond with guanine bases. These pairings are referred to as "base pairs" and form the basis for coding information in DNA. Each molecule of DNA contains a huge amount of information encoded by as many as 250 million base pairs.

DNA is stored on chromosomes within the nucleus. A thin membrane separates the interior portion of the nucleus from the cytoplasm of the cell. Like the cell wall and cell membrane, the plasma membrane that surrounds the nucleus allows certain materials to flow in and out of the nucleus. These membranes, which allow certain materials to flow through them while they protect the cell from the surrounding environment, are known as **semipermeable membranes** or **selectively permeable membranes**. Because large particles need to move in and out of a cell, the nuclear membrane contains many pores that allow these oversized materials to pass through.

The genetic material essential for life processes are stored inside the nucleus. However, this separation of genetic materials within the confines of a nuclear membrane does not occur in all cells. In some cells, like those of bacteria, genetic materials float freely inside the cytoplasm of the cell. Cells without a nuclear membrane are known as **prokaryotes**. In plant and animal cells, however, the genetic information is located within the nucleus, which is separated from the rest of the cell by the nuclear membrane. Cells that have a well-defined nucleus are known as **eukaryotes**, or eukaryotic cells.

Since plant cells are eukaryotic, they have a well-developed nucleus with a membrane that stores all of the genetic information within it. This genetic information is located on the long, thin, coiled strands of DNA called chromosomes. Chromosomes provide the cell with information regarding all the processes of life—how to make proteins, when to reproduce, how to grow, and so on. In most eukaryotic cells, chromosomes are a combination of proteins and DNA and are tightly coiled so that they take up less space in the nucleus. These coiled masses of chromosomes are known as **chromatin**.

The nucleus of the cell contains long strands of a thin substance called **nuclear lamina**. Nuclear lamina gives the nucleus of the cell the structure and support needed to maintain its shape. The lamina within the nucleus works in a similar fashion to the mooring lines on a boat. A lamina anchors itself to the interior portion of the double-layered nuclear membrane and stretches throughout the nucleus in a network of interwoven lines. The nuclear lamina also plays an essential role in the process of cellular reproduction.

Also located within the nucleus is a small, dark mass known as the nucleolus. The nucleolus does not have a membrane that surrounds it like the nucleus does, and it exists within the boundaries of the nucleus.

The nucleus plays a vital role in the life of a plant cell. The most important role that the nucleus plays is to produce ribosomal ribonucleic acid (rRNA), which is used in cell replication and needed to create ribosomes to be used for protein production. In addition, each nucleus contains a tremendous amount of information that is essential to the life of the plant. All the information a plant needs to react to its environment, grow, reproduce, and synthesize food is stored within the DNA of plants.

Scientists today are also realizing that the DNA of plants can be altered to help mankind. Geneticists have learned how to modify plant genetics to better suit our needs. We now have the ability to produce plants that are resistant to drought, disease, and herbicides, thanks to our increased understanding of DNA in plant cells. These modified plants have increased food production around the world. Botanists and geneticists continue to look for new ways to modify the genes in plants to help improve our lives.

3

How the Organelles
of the Cell
Work Together

The cell wall and cell membrane work to protect and support the cell. The nucleus contains all of the genetic materials required to undergo the processes of life in the cell, including making food, growth, and reproduction. Cells rely on a variety of other specialized organelles to carry out the processes of life.

Our heart must beat in order for us to survive. However, our heart would not be able to keep us alive if our liver did not clean toxins from our body. We also could not survive without the organs of our digestive system that allow us to break down food and take in nutrients. The cell works in much the same way. The complex relationships between organelles in the cell allow for the production of proteins, the production of food, and the removal of wastes.

Inside the cell there are a variety of organelles suspended in a fluid called cytoplasm. These organelles help the plant carry out the functions required for survival. The survival of the plant cell requires an organized team effort.

CYTOPLASM AND CYSTOL

Robert Hooke believed that plant cells shared a type of circulatory system similar to ours that he believed scientists would be able to explain if they were "helped by better microscopes." Two centuries later, scientists like Matthias Schleiden, who were using more advanced microscopic equipment, were able to distinguish that there were a variety of materials moving within the cell. The next question for these scientists would clearly be: What kind of material were these materials moving around in?

Today, all of the materials within the cell membrane, except for the nucleus, are collectively referred to as the cytoplasm. The cytoplasm is made up of two separate parts. First is the **cystol**. The cystol is the fluid matrix within the cell that is not enclosed within organelle membranes. It is a viscous fluid made primarily of water, which accounts for almost three-quarters of the content of the cystol solution. The remaining portion is made up of ions and insoluble materials that float within the cystol itself like crystals. This portion also contains oil droplets, as well as the proteins that make up the cytoskeleton (the filaments inside the cell that maintain its structure). Scientists have found that cystol is more viscous than water. Viscosity is a liquid's resistance to tangential movement. Materials that have a high viscosity, such as oils, are thicker and slower to spread out over a surface. For instance, a drop of water falling on a table spreads out quickly, while a drop of honey on the same table spreads out more slowly. Therefore, honey—like cystol—is more viscous, and therefore thicker, than water.

The other portion of the cytoplasm is made up of the organelles. Organelles in the cytoplasm are separated from the fluid cystol that surrounds them by thin membranes. Many organelles are important to cell function, including Golgi bodies, **mitochondria** (singular: mitochondrion), and ribosomes, which all have specific functions to carry out in the cell. Together, the cystol and the organelles combine to form the cytoplasm of the cell. The cytoplasm is where almost all of the functions necessary to the life of the cell take place.

ENDOPLASMIC RETICULUM

A group of cell biologists working with an electron microscope in the 1940s were puzzled when they observed what appeared to be a long, folded membrane within the embryo of a chicken egg. (The electron microscope they were using allowed them to examine objects that were too small to appear on traditional microscopes.) The scientists were puzzled by the intricate, wavy membrane that they found floating within the cell. Earlier scientists had also written about unknown membranes found within the cell, but the electron microscope now allowed them to examine this unknown material more closely.

One of these scientists was Albert Claude. In the 1920s, Claude began to study the chemical composition of this folded material, which he called a microsome. Claude found that the microsome was made up mostly of lipids. Three years later, the microsome was renamed the endoplasmic reticulum.

The endoplasmic reticulum comes in a variety of different forms and performs many functions within the cell. All the different forms of endoplasmic reticulum (ER) are made of networks of flattened membranous disks, which are called cisternae. These disks are connected by tubes called vesicles and tubules. This collection of membranous disks and tubes are folded and twisted into the "ribbons," or ER. Claude made these observations about the structure of ER in 1945.

There are two basic types of ER found in plant cells. The first, called rough endoplasmic reticulum (RER), is so named because its surface is covered with small spherical ribosomes. **Ribosomes** are the components in the cell that make proteins. Ribosomes build proteins for the cell by reading the encoded messages in RNA, which acts like a blueprint, and constructing proteins from their building blocks, which are called amino acids. Scientists originally thought that the "spots" on ER, which we now know to be ribosomes, were permanent. Such is not the case. Ribosomes are not permanently attached to the surface of the RER, but at any given time, many ribosomes will be attached to the RER, making the RER look studded or bumpy. The surface of the RER serves as a work bench where ribosomes construct the various proteins required by the cell. The folds of the RER create more space for the ribosomes to construct proteins.

As proteins are made by the ribosomes on the surface, RER arranges these protein chains and begins the work of transporting the protein toward its final destination. The RER is assisted in this process by the **Golgi apparatus**, one of the other organelles found within the cell.

RER also serves to produce other materials in specialized cells. Pancreatic cells, for instance, have specialized RER that produces insulin, a hormone that is responsible for controlling the breakdown of sugars in the body.

Smooth endoplasmic reticulum (SER) looks very similar to RER except for the fact that the ribosomes that give RER its name are missing in SER. The basic structure of SER resembles that of RER very closely though, appearing as folded membranes when viewed under high magnification. SER serves a variety of different roles within the cell and its function varies depending upon the type of cell in which it is found.

In plant cells, the lipids required to form cell membranes and other key parts of the cell are built, or synthesized, by the SER using basic units called fatty acids. Fatty acids are long chains of carbon, hydrogen, and oxygen that are held together by chemical bonds. These fatty acids can be turned into lipids, which are a form of fat. Fat is not always bad, though. Both plants and animals require fats to live. In plant cells, fatty acids are constructed in the plastids within the cell and are turned to lipids by the SER. The SER also aids in the breakdown of lipids, as well. The function of the SER may also include the movement of materials within the cell, the break down of carbohydrates, and the removal of dangerous toxins.

Both the SER and RER share the same basic structure. Both are infolded membranes that act as work benches within the plant cell. The SER and RER are both anchored to the outer membrane of the nucleus as well.

GOLGI APPARATUS

Before the early twentieth century, scientists were aware of the existence of a series of interconnected sacs and membranes that appeared somewhat similar in shape to the endoplasmic reticulum. They gave this unidentified material many names as they worked to identify the parts of the cell. One of the names given to this organelle was the canaliculi. Others names for it were trophospongium, the osmiophilic platelets, and the dictyosomes.

A group of scientists in the 1920s and 1930s, however, recognized that all of these structures were actually the same structure that looked slightly different in different types of cells. By the 1940s, many cell scientists had agreed on a name for the organelle—the Golgi apparatus. This name was given in honor of the Italian scientist Camillo Golgi, who was the first to describe the odd folded membranes in animal cells in the late nineteenth century.

There were still skeptics in the scientific world, however. Our understanding of biology and chemistry grew tremendously during the early twentieth century when there were many more scientists than ever before and microscopes were becoming more advanced. The scientific community demanded definite proof that the so-called Golgi apparatus seen in animal cells was the same as the folded, pinched membranes that appeared in plant cells. Any scientist with a quality microscope could plainly see that the organelle that scientists labeled the Golgi looked different in plant and animal cells. Did they both serve the same purpose?

Scientists Keith Porter, Roger Buvat, and E. Perner finally successfully documented the Golgi apparatus in plant cells and identified it as the same organelle with much the same function as the Golgi found in animal cells in a 1957 paper that the scientists coauthored. Other scientists finally agreed that although they looked slightly different from each, the Golgi of plant and animal cells shared a common purpose in the life of the cell.

When viewed under high-power magnification, the Golgi in most plant cells resemble layers of membranes placed one atop another in a way that vaguely resembles a stack of pancakes. Each of the separate layers or stacks on the Golgi is called a dictyosome. These stacks are all bound together by thin layers of membranes. Most Golgi appear to have between four and seven flattened membrane sections called cisternae that are stacked atop one another. Like other membranes, the Golgi is comprised mostly of lipids, or fats.

The Golgi apparatus functions as a shipping dock, moving materials from one area to another inside the cell. In some cases, the Golgi will prepare materials, specifically proteins and carbohydrates created in the cell, for shipment outside of the boundaries of the cell wall. Many of these materials are proteins that are built by the endoplasmic reticulum. However, the Golgi also helps to move other large **macromolecules**, which are highly specialized molecules. Besides moving proteins, the Golgi also serves to move lipids and carbohydrates. Plant Golgi tend to move more carbohydrates than animal cells because plants are constantly producing and consuming these carbohydrates throughout their life cycle.

Macromolecules are transported to their final destination by sugars that carry these materials throughout the cell. These materials direct intracellular movement of the molecule, acting in much the same way that an address does on a package you send through the mail. They are also responsible for moving materials outside the cell if the macromolecule is prescribed to go elsewhere. Materials destined to be shipped out of the Golgi are placed in vesicles that aid in the transport of these materials to their final destination. The Golgi not only sends finished proteins, carbohydrates, and other macromolecules out after they are built, but it also breaks down proteins that are not working and sends them back for repairs. As the plant develops and its needs change, the role of the Golgi changes as well.

The membranes that make up the Golgi have either a negative or positive charge. For this reason, the Golgi has two separate regions on either end. One region, which is closest to the ER and is thicker, is known as the "cis-face" of the Golgi. The portion of the Golgi that is farthest away from the ER has the thickest cisternae and is known as the "trans-face" of the Golgi. Scientists use these terms to describe the location and function of the different cisternae that make up the Golgi.

The Golgi also serves a variety of specialized functions that are specific to plant cells. For example, have you ever seen a Venus fly trap or a pitcher plant? These plants are insectivores, meaning they capture and consume insects. The enzymes required to break down the insect's body are produced in the Golgi apparatus. The Golgi is also responsible for releasing the enzyme that helps break down the cell wall and produces mucilage that thickens root caps during growth.

MITOCHONDRIA

What do you think of when you hear the term *respiration*? For most people, the term makes them think of the act of breathing, of inhaling air, and exhaling carbon dioxide. However, while it is true that the term is often used in these ways, respiration in cell biology has a completely different meaning. The intake and output of gases is essential to cellular respiration in both plants and animals, but it is not the *whole* function.

Cellular respiration is the process of making cellular energy that the cell can use to carry out life functions. The main product of cellular respiration is called **adenosine triphosphate (ATP)**. ATP is the cellular source of energy. Without it, a cell would not be able to carry out the functions essential for life, and it would die.

It took scientists some time to fully understand the process of respiration. It was obvious enough that humans required oxygen to live. But why is it that oxygen is necessary?

The answer came when advances in cellular biology allowed scientists to better understand the nature of cells. When it became obvious that each cell was alive and undergoing the processes of life, it became clearer that the air we breathe, and what we commonly call "respiration," was serving some purpose on a cellular level.

Edward Pfluger (1829–1910) was the first scientist to state that respiration was a process that took place in the cell, giving us the term *cellular respiration*. *Cellular respiration* is a somewhat misleading term because all forms of respiration ultimately end in processes that occur within the cell and therefore all respiration that occurs in living organisms is cellular respiration. Pfluger also stated that it was not just animals that respired on a cellular level. He believed that plants also respired.

WHAT'S THAT SMELL?

Flowers typically make us think of beautiful bouquets and sweet fragrances. In fact, most flowers use bright colors and pleasant aromas to attract the species of animals, birds, and insects that pollinate them. One rare flower, however, has neither a pleasant odor nor bright flowers. In fact, this flower smells like rotted meat. Nicknamed the "corpse flower" or "carrion flower," the flower officially named titan arum (*Amorphophallus titanum*) is not only striking because of its smell. Its huge dark purple petals may stretch up to six feet (1.8 m) across, making it stand out from the bright pink, blue, and orange flowers that grow in its native Sumatra, an island in Indonesia. The petals surround a huge cone-shaped spire that is actually made up of smaller flowers that emit the powerful odor.

This giant flower is one of the world's most unique flower specimens. It is believed to only bloom for a few days every few years, unfurling its petals and emitting the odor of death in an effort to attract pollinators, such as beetles and carrion flies, that believe they are feasting on rotting meat. Instead, they wind up covered in pollen grains when they land on the plant's tall central cone. The insects then fly away to other locations and possibly spread the pollen of one carrion flower to another.

Titan arums are prized by botanists for their rarity and immense size. Plant lovers wait for years to witness the unfurling of the flower, an event that may only last for a few days.

(opposite page) Figure 3.1 Titan arum is a member of the *Araceae* family, which includes plants such as the calla lily and philodendron.

Once scientists began to accept Pfluger's conclusions, questions began to arise about respiration in cells. What was the purpose of cell respiration? What did cells require to breathe? Where in the cell did respiration take place?

As occurred with the Golgi apparatus, different scientists discovered the mitochondria at different times and most of them gave it their

own name. Vibrioden, chondriokonts, chromidia and polioplasma were all early names for the organelle we now know as the mitochondria. At one time, the mitochondria had over two dozen different names, further confusing scientists who were trying to sort out what respiration was and how it occurred. It seemed that every cell biologist had their own idea about how cells underwent respiration, and all of them were scrambling to find the real answers to the questions regarding respiration.

In 1900, cell biologist Leonor Michaelis was testing the reaction of different cell organelles to dyes. When he injected an animal cell with Janus green B dye, he was shocked to see that the small, newly described mitochondria were still clear and untouched by the dye. This was because mitochondria had the ability to oxidize, or break down, the dye. Michaelis tested plant cells and found that they too had mitochondria that oxidized Janus green. This proved that the mitochondrion was a unique organelle, and that it existed in the cells of both plants and animals.

It was not until the 1940s that scientists truly began to understand the significance of mitochondria, when cell biologist Albert Claude used a centrifuge to isolate organelles in the cell responsible for respiration. He found that the mitochondria were responsible for respiration in the cell. This was a breakthrough because up until that time, scientists believed

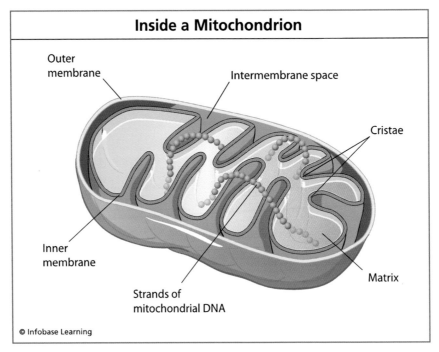

FIGURE 3.2 Mitochondria supply the cell with the ATP needed to perform activities. Mitochondria are surrounded by two separate membranes. The inner membrane has many folds, called cristae, which increase the surface area for ATP production. The matrix, enclosed by the inner membrane, is an enzyme-rich fluid.

that the nucleus, which was the most clearly visible organelle in the cell, was responsible for cellular respiration.

The development of electron microscopes gave scientists their first real look at the structure of mitochondria. They found that while the mitochondria appeared to be a round or oblong organelle with a membrane surrounding it, there was actually a network of membranes folded within the outer membrane. These inner membranes, which appear like a piece of paper folded many times and stuffed into a ball, became known as **cristae**. It was later discovered that the cristae membrane is actually an extension of the interior membrane of the mitochondria. These cristae are surrounded by an open area in the mitochondria called the matrix. It is within the cristae and matrix of the mitochondria that ATP production occurs.

Mitochondrial membranes are made of specialized proteins and lipids and contain small channel proteins called porins that allow materials to pass through the membrane. Most plant cells have thousands of mitochondria inside of them, although the number and percentage of mitochondria varies from cell to cell. Mitochondria typically make up about 10% of the cytoplasm in a normal plant cell. Oftentimes, the mitochondria in a cell are positioned close to sites where energy is needed or where sugars are stored for energy use by the plant. In the leaves of most trees, mitochondria within the cells are usually located in close proximity to the chloroplasts so that sunlight can rapidly be converted to energy.

One unique characteristic of mitochondria is that the DNA shared by all of the other parts of the plant is not the same DNA found within the mitochondria. Mitochondrial DNA is completely unique and some scientists have hypothesized that the mitochondria of the cell were originally symbiotic bacteria that lived within the cell and made energy many millions of years ago. Over time, these bacteria became part of the cell but kept their own DNA.

The process by which mitochondria make energy is known as the Krebs cycle, named after German scientist Hans Adolf Krebs. Krebs wanted to determine how it was that mitochondria could take carbohydrates and turn them into a usable energy source in ATP. Krebs outlined the complex reactions involved in ATP production in 1937 while working as a biochemist at Cambridge University in England. Today, the Krebs cycle is also known as the citric acid cycle.

Although the production of ATP is the main function of mitochondria, they also play other roles within the plant cell. Mitochondria also conserve energy and will slow down production in reaction to the conditions around the plant. Mitochondria also play an important part in **apoptosis**, or prescribed cell death. As in animals, cells have a certain life span in plants and, therefore, they eventually die. The mitochondria play a vital role by initiating this process and causing the cell to die so it can be replaced by younger, healthier cells.

The main function of mitochondria, however, is the production of energy for the cell. The production of ATP will be discussed later.

RIBOSOMES

As we have already discussed, ribosomes play a vital role in the production of proteins on the endoplasmic reticulum. However, ribosomes are not strictly bound to the ER. Some scientists, in fact, considered ribosomes to be their own separate organelle within the cell. Others argue that because the ribosome does not have a membrane that surrounds it, the ribosome cannot be classified as an organelle.

Regardless of whether or not it can be classified as an organelle, ribosomes play an absolutely essential role in the cell. Ribosomes on the RER use information brought from the DNA within the nucleus to the ribosome by specialized nucleic acids called messenger ribonucleic acids or mRNA. The ribosomes then take the "message," which includes information about protein production, and begin the process of assembling long chains of molecules called polypeptides into proteins.

Ribosomes are actually made of proteins and RNA themselves. They are very small (20 nanometers), even by the standards of cell organelles. Ribosomes actually have two parts, or subunits, that assist each other during protein production. In eukaryotic cells, the subunits of ribosomes are referred to as the 60-s subunit and the 40-s subunit. The 60-s subunit is the larger of the two. These parts work in unison to gather information from mRNA and then assemble the amino acids necessary to correctly build the protein. The ribosomes that build these proteins can either be "free" or floating in the cytoplasm of the cell, or they can be "membrane bound" like those that build proteins on the RER.

ACTIN, INTERMEDIATE FILAMENTS, AND MICROTUBULES

Several filaments within the cytoplasm act as a framework for the interior of the cell. This group of filaments is known as the cytoskeleton, and they work in the cell much as our skeletons work for us. The cytoskeleton gives the cell support and helps organize the structure of the internal portion of the cell. Actin filaments act like chains or ropes within the cell. They give the cell its basic interior integrity. Intermediate fibers also act in the same way, although they are thicker than actin filaments. Together, the actin and intermediate fibers allow the cell to expand when it absorbs water from the surrounding environment. Another type of filament called microtubules prevents the cell from being crushed by the pressure around it.

If a cell works like a factory, then actin, intermediate fibers, and microtubules form the factory's inner structure and framework. Like strong I-beams that span across a large building, intermediate fibers support the basic shape of the plant cell, help it to maintain its integrity, and protect it from being compressed.

OTHER PLASTIDS

Amyloplasts

Amyloplasts function to store starch and exist only in certain plant cells. They are classified as plastids, the same category that chloroplasts are in. Amyloplasts occur mostly in plants that contain a great deal of starch. Starch is a polysaccharide sugar made up of long chains or simple sugars. These long chains can be stored by a plant and then used when sugars need to be broken down for ATP production. Amyloplasts act like a plant's cabinet or pantry. They store food so that the plant can utilize the energy when the need arises.

The amyloplast also directs root growth. Root caps in plants contain a large number of amyloplasts and because amyloplasts are very dense, they work their way to the bottom of the cell, encouraging the cell to grow in a certain direction (against gravity). In the case of roots, amyloplasts promote what is known as positive gravitropsim. In other words, gravity causes the plant to grow in the direction in which it pulls.

Chromoplasts

Have you ever stopped to examine the variety of colors that are contained in flower petals? Have you ever wondered why the ripened fruit of an apple tree turns from green to red? This is caused by a special type of plastid called a chromoplast. **Chromoplasts** are plastids inside the plant cell that are responsible for pigment storage. Plants use pigments for a variety of reasons. Flowers, for example, have brightly colored petals to attract insects that will carry their pollen from one plant to the next for fertilization. Chromoplasts provide the pigment that is needed to attract insects, birds, and other pollinators. Chromoplasts store many of the pigments in plants that we see in the fall when the leaves are changing color.

Proteinoplasts

Proteinoplasts are unique to plant cells and, like other plastids, they store materials that the plant needs. Proteinoplasts store proteins for use by the plant. They are most commonly found in nuts like peanuts. Although proteinoplasts were discovered in the 1960s, very little is still known about how these specialized plastids assist the plant.

REACTIONS INSIDE CELL WALLS

At any given moment, there are thousands of reactions going on within a plant cell. Vacuoles clean up and gather waste to prepare it for shipment out of the cell and also maintain turgor pressure. The nucleus gives orders for protein synthesis, which sets the RER and ribosomes in motion, locking amino acids together in long polypeptide chains that the Golgi apparatus identifies, tags, and ships. Inside the chloroplasts, sunlight is being converted to sugars that the plant can use. Mitochondria churn out ATP so that the entire process can continue. Plastids move starches and pigments to different locations within the cell. The cell membrane selects which materials cannot go in or out of the cell. The cell walls provide structural support outside the cell, while actin and other cytoskeletal filaments provide internal structure. Even though plants appear still when we look at them, thousands of different processes are occurring simultaneously within the plant that allow it to survive. However, none of these processes we are about to discuss would be possible without the cooperation that occurs within the boundaries of the cell wall.

4

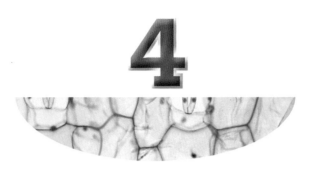

Photosynthesis

When scientists began studying and observing plant cells, one of the first questions they asked was how plants collected the energy they required to undergo life processes. Even before Robert Hooke discovered the cell, humans were fascinated by plants. Early man puzzled at how plants, which were rooted in the ground and could not move, nevertheless managed to find food. Even the earliest scientists knew that plants were alive. They were born, they grew, they produced offspring, and they died. So how did they find food?

The first scientist who conducted recorded experiments on how plants found food was Jan Baptista van Helmont (1579–1644), a Belgian scientist who studied the soil in which plants lived. Van Helmont concluded that since plants did not consume food the way that animals did, they must find their nutrients in the soil. To determine whether or not this was correct, he carefully weighed a plant's soil as it grew. Van Helmont soon made two observations: First, the weight of the soil changed very little, even when the plant grew a great deal; second, the main factor affecting the change in the weight of the soil was how much moisture was present.

Thus, it turned out that plants did not get their nutrients from the soil. In that case, where did these nutrients come from? Early scientists, like van Helmont, knew that there were certain things that a plant required to survive. Without oxygen, water, and sunlight, whatever plant they tested would soon die.

FIGURE 4.1 Belgian physician and biochemist Jan Baptista van Helmont first introduced the term *gas*.

Later scientists, including Englishman Joseph Priestly, began to test the effects of plants on gases in a controlled environment. It was discovered that the oxygen that living things, such as mice, used during respiration came from plants. It became clear to scientists that plants created oxygen as a byproduct of their respiration.

It was Swiss scientist Jean Senebier that first deduced that plants not only produced oxygen but also used carbon dioxide while undergoing the process of respiration in the late eighteenth century. Senebier also believed that the processes of respiration occurred exclusively in the parts of the plant where green chloroplasts appeared. Although Senebier didn't completely understand the process, he was beginning to piece together the processes that make up photosynthesis. Photosynthesis is the process by which organisms, like plants, convert carbon dioxide gas into sugars—plants' main energy source—through the use of the radiant energy in sunlight.

In the late 1920s, a young American scientist named Cornelius Bernardus van Niel (1897–1985) became the first scientist to explain

PLANT FAT

Like animals, plants rely on stores of energy-rich fats. However, plant fats do not resemble the fats that we typically recognize. Plant fats are unsaturated fats. All fats are comprised of triglycerides, which are chemical compounds made of a glycerol backbone and fatty acid chains. These fatty acid chains have long strands of carbons surrounded by hydrogen atoms. If these hydrocarbon chains are completely filled with hydrogen atoms, then the fat is known as a saturated fat.

Saturated fats are the type of fats that animals store and are solid at room temperature. Saturated fats appear as the white portion of a cooked steak (also known as the gristle). Plant fats, however, are unsaturated fats with hydrocarbon chains that are not completely filled with hydrogen atoms. Because of this, unsaturated fats are liquid at room temperature and may not be immediately recognizable as fats. Olive oil, canola oil, and vegetable oil are all examples of unsaturated plant fats. Olive oil, in particular, is recommended as a substitute for other fats in the diet because olive oil does not accumulate in blood vessels the way that saturated animal fats do. This reduces the chance of heart disease and stroke among those who eat a diet rich in olive oils.

the process of chemical photosynthesis. Van Niel was born in Denmark and later immigrated to the United States with his parents. While working at Stanford University in California, he began examining algae as they underwent photosynthesis and pieced together the elements necessary for plants to undergo photosynthesis.

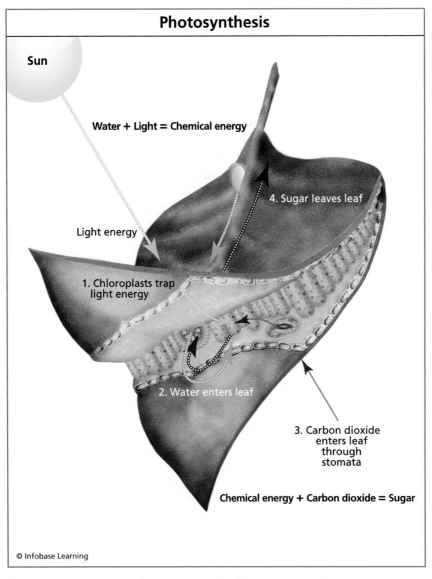

FIGURE 4.2 In photosynthesis, carbon dioxide is converted into organic compounds, including sugars, using light energy.

Van Niel realized that plant cells, in which photosynthesis actually takes place, captured radiant energy from the Sun and used carbon dioxide gas and water to produce sugars. These sugars were used to fuel the plant. A byproduct of the photosynthetic process was oxygen. This would explain why Priestly found that mice, which would die if left in a sealed glass jar with no oxygen, could survive in that same glass jar if plants were present. The oxygen produced by the plant was enough to keep the mouse alive.

It may seem strange that carbon dioxide, which is a gas, could ever be used to make sugar. However, the reality is that from a chemical standpoint, many of the building blocks of sugars are found in carbon dioxide. Carbon dioxide's chemical formula (CO_2) is not that different than the formula for a basic carbohydrate (CH_2O). To transform carbon dioxide to a sugar, or carbohydrate, plants need hydrogen. This hydrogen comes from water (H_2O). However, simply placing carbon dioxide and water together does not make a carbohydrate. The atoms that make up these compounds must be reconstructed into sugars. These reactions will not occur without some source of energy to drive them. That energy comes from sunlight. The term photosynthesis is actually a combination of the Greek words *photo*, which means "light" and *synthesis* which means "to build" or "construct." During photosynthesis, food is "built" by using energy drawn from light.

The process of photosynthesis begins within the plant cell. Chloroplasts, which are organelles specific to plants (as described earlier), are where the first steps of photosynthesis take place. Recall that in chloroplasts, there are stacks of green plates that look like pancakes, which are called granum. These grana are covered in a membrane that is called the **thylakoid membrane**. Most of photosynthesis occurs within the thylakoid membranes.

Sunlight is essential to photosynthesis, and it must be captured by colored pigments. The most common pigment in plant cells in chlorophyll. Chlorophyll pigment gives plants their green color, and it is most common in leaves and portions of the plant that are exposed to sunlight. However, chlorophyll is not the only pigment found in plants. Orange carotene pigments and yellow xanthophylls are also found in plants and help to capture more sunlight. It is important to understand, though, that pigments like chlorophyll appear the color they do because they reflect certain colors of light. Light waves in the **visible spectrum**, or the range of colors visible to our eyes, come in seven colors. You are probably aware that a rainbow consists of seven colors. The most common way to remember these colors is the mnemonic "ROY G BIV": red, orange, yellow, green, blue, indigo and violet. These colors are also represent the visible spectrum.

We see colors because different wavelengths of energy produce different colors of light. Plants use a variety of pigments like chlorophyll and carotenes to absorb rays from the Sun and use their energy. Chlorophyll appears green because it absorbs all colors of light *except* green. Therefore the energy found in red, orange, yellow, blue, indigo, and violet light is absorbed and used as fuel to turn carbon dioxide into sugar for use by plants. We actually incorrectly associate the color green with plants. Most plants appear green because they are unable to absorb green light for use in energy production.

Photosynthesis does not always occur at the same rates in plants. Outside factors can affect the rate of photosynthesis and sugar production by reducing the effectiveness of enzymes within the plant cell. Temperature is one important factor in the rate of photosynthesis. The enzymes in plants associated with the photosynthetic process function much better in temperatures that are above freezing (32°F; 0°C) than in colder temperatures. Photosynthesis can still occur in below-freezing temperatures, but it occurs much more slowly. The amount of available light also affects photosynthesis rates. Dark, cloudy days reduce the number of light photons that reach the leaves and slow down the process of photosynthesis. Very dry conditions slow down the photosynthetic process, as well, although some plants like cacti and crabgrass have adapted to dry conditions and can undergo photosynthesis with minimal available water.

Scientists discovered that photosynthesis actually occurs in two separate and distinct stages. These stages are known as the light-dependent reactions and light-independent reactions. They are most often simply referred to as light reactions and dark reactions.

LIGHT REACTIONS

In plants, most of the photosynthetic process takes place within leaves. More specifically, it takes place in the interior portion of the leaf known as the **mesophyll** (which means "middle leaf" in Greek). The upper and lower surface portions of a leaf, which are known as the epidermis, have almost nothing to do with photosynthesis. Most of the chloroplasts in a plant cell are found in the mesophyll. In the mesophyll, the pigments within a plant collect energy from **photons**. Photons are the basic unit of light energy.

THE CASE OF THE DEAD HORSES: PLANT POISONS

Kentucky is horse country. The state takes great pride in its rich history of raising and training some of the best thoroughbred racehorses in the world. The countryside around Lexington, Kentucky, is dominated by white board fence and massive barns where the next generation of racehorses is being bred and raised. However, in the early 2000s, thoroughbred foals began mysteriously dying at farms across the state. At first, no one had any idea what could have been responsible for the deaths of these prized foals. Some even believed that foul play was involved.

Scientists soon found out what was responsible for the deaths of so many foals. Small insect larvae, known as tent caterpillars, were indirectly responsible for the death of young horses across Kentucky and in neighboring states, as well. You may have seen the nests that tent caterpillars form in the branches of trees. They look like very thick, matted "tents" made of white strings, similar to spider silk.

Foals eating grass sometimes inadvertently ate caterpillars and then died from ingesting the cyanide contained in the larvae. However, the cyanide was not produced by the larvae themselves. Instead, the larvae ingested this deadly toxin from the leaves of wild cherry trees that grew in the area. Cherry trees contain cyanide as a defensive chemical, and the caterpillars—immune to the effects of the toxin—spread the deadly poison to the horses that ate them. In response, horse owners killed the tent caterpillars with insecticides so that they wouldn't spread the toxin when they left the nest to travel across the ground. After the horse death mystery was solved, farmers also began removing cherry trees from the woods that surrounded their pastures. The deaths stopped, but not before many foals died.

When chloroplasts collect light, they use the resulting energy to build the compound known as ATP, or adenosine triphosphate. ATP is the basic unit of energy within a cell. Energy from sunlight causes electrons located on the hydrogen atoms in water to jump to higher energy levels farther away from the nucleus of the atom. Eventually, the electron begins to return to its original position, and as it does so, energy is released. This energy is used to form the elements necessary for photosynthesis. This formation occurs in two phases known as photosystem I and photosystem II. As the electron returns to its normal state after being excited by the photon, the release of energy occurs along what is known as the **electron transport chain (ETC)**. The ETC provides the necessary energy that the plant needs to convert adenosine diphosphate (ADP) to ATP by adding a phosphate. (ADP is a similar phosphate compound to ATP but contains only 2 phosphates instead of 3.) These phosphate bonds may not seem all that important, but they serve as an energy source for the plant cell. Like a battery, the phosphate bonds in ATP contain energy that is released when needed. For example, when we turn the key to start our cars, the action releases the energy stored inside the battery. When plants need to make sugar, energy is available to them in the form of ATP.

Another molecule besides ATP plays an important role in the light reactions. This molecule is called nicotinamide adenine dinucleotide phosphate, or NADP+. (The plus sign indicates that NADP has lost an electron and will be able to accept one.) This electron comes from water, which has a chemical formula of H_2O. The hydrogen (H) from water attaches to NADP+ to form a compound known as NADPH. NADPH is essential for the next step in the photosynthetic process, which is known as the dark reactions.

So far in the process, the plant has required two elements to complete the light reactions. Those elements are photons of sunlight, which produce energy to start the light reactions, and water to turn NADP+ to NADPH. Both ATP and NADPH will be important in the upcoming dark reactions, but what about the water molecule that offered a hydrogen to NADP+? After the hydrogen was removed, all that remained of the water molecule were two atoms of oxygen. These atoms of oxygen bond together to form the molecule O_2, which is the form of oxygen gas that we breathe. The process of photosynthesis, therefore, is essential for living things because it produces the oxygen that we breathe. That oxygen, in turn, allows our cells to convert the sugar that we consume into energy. Plants, therefore, are vital to our survival. When we water plants growing in a garden, we are actually fueling the first essential step of photosynthesis. We are also benefitting ourselves since the plant will only use the hydrogen from each water molecule and will release the oxygen back into the air for us to breathe.

DARK REACTIONS

The first stage of photosynthesis is called the light reaction phase because it occurs in the thylakoid membrane and requires light to operate. The second stage, however, occurs within the thick jellylike fluid that surrounds the stacks of grana. This fluid is called the stroma, and, as indicated by the term *dark reactions*, these reactions that take place here do not require light energy to fuel them because ATP contains stored energy that fuels the dark reactions. Whereas the light reactions occur mainly during the hours of brightest light, the dark reactions can occur at any time.

In dark reactions, CO_2 is converted to the sugar glucose, which has a chemical formula of $C_6H_{12}O_6$. The creation of glucose is the purpose of the entire photosynthetic process because glucose is the plant's food source. As you can see from its chemical formula, glucose contains carbon, hydrogen, and oxygen. The carbon and oxygen needed to form these sugars are provided by the CO_2, and the hydrogen required to build glucose comes from the NADPH that is produced during the light reactions.

The dark reactions, also known as the Calvin cycle or the Calvin-Benson cycle, begin when a molecule of CO_2 enters the stroma and joins with a 5-carbon molecule known as ribulose bisphosphate (RuBP). RuBP is a molecule that is formed within the stroma during the production of glucose. When the RuBP and CO_2 combine, they form a 6-carbon compound that is similar to glucose. However, this 6-carbon molecule is unstable and breaks down into two 3-carbon compounds that are known as phosphoglycerates.

It requires 6 CO_2 molecules to combine with six molecules of 5-carbon RuBP to start one Calvin cycle. The CO_2 and RuBP combine to form six 6-carbon molecules that immediately break down into 12 molecules of the 3-carbon compound known as phosphoglycerate. At this point, the energy stored in ATP and the hydrogen of NADPH is needed. With the energy available from these 2 compounds that were created in the light reactions, the 12 molecules of phosphoglycerate are turned into 12 molecules of a compound known as glyceraldehyde 3-phosphate. This is the step that the entire Calvin cycle has been leading to since two of these glyceraldehyde 3-phosphates can be combined to form one molecule of glucose, the sugar that the plant uses for energy. The remainder of the glyceraldehyde 3-phosphate is converted to additional RuBP using energy in ATP. This constant regeneration of RuBP allows the cycle to occur once again.

In short, the Calvin cycle uses the energy available in ATP and NADPH to turn carbon dioxide into sugar that the plant needs to survive. The energy source for this process comes from sunlight. The NADP+ and ADP that have used up their energy in the Calvin cycle are recharged with light energy along the electron transport chain and can once again provide the energy necessary to turn the glyceraldehyde 3-phosphate into sugar. The hydrogen in water is also required to fuel photosynthesis, but the oxygen molecules in water are not necessary and are therefore released as a byproduct of photosynthesis. This is very important to us since the oxygen produced by plants allows us to survive.

C_4 AND CAM PATHWAYS

Have you ever looked at a patch of dry grass after a long period without rain and seen a single weed growing in the center that was still bright green while all the other plants around it are brown and dry? Or have you ever noticed that during those same dry periods, some plants, such as corn, remain healthy and seem to be far less affected by the weather than other plants?

There is a reason that plants such as crabgrass, millet, and corn maintain their healthy green color while most other plants (besides cacti and succulents) become brown and dry due to a lack of water. You have just read about the processes of photosynthesis that occur in plant cells. However, some plant cells are able to undergo slightly different methods to produce sugar.

Plants take in CO_2 during the initial stages of photosynthesis. As a result, one of the initial products that the plant makes is the compound known as glyceraldehyde 3-phosphate. Because they use 3-carbon molecules to make sugar during photosynthesis, these plants are referred to as C_3 plants. These C_3 plants undergo photosynthesis as described above. However, two Australian scientists working in the 1960s discovered that other plants have adapted a method that allows them to manipulate the initial carbon compound into a 4-carbon compound known as oxaloacetate. Plants like corn and crabgrass have the ability to fix four carbons together in this manner. Any plant that creates oxaloacetate instead of glyceraldehyde 3-phosphate is known as a C_4 plant rather than a C_3 plant because of the four carbons found in oxaloacetate.

What is the advantage of going through this process? Why would a plant want to adapt a method that is different than most other plants? The advantage of the C_4 method of photosynthesis does not become apparent until periods of high heat and low moisture have begun to turn plants brown and dry. In late summer, extended dry periods cause plants to close their stomata. Stomata are openings in the leaf, usually on the underside, that allow the entrance of gases and water into the leaf interior. These openings can close during periods of drought so that water from inside the plant will not be lost. The problem, however, is that closed stomata also prevent carbon dioxide from entering the leaf. As you learned earlier, carbon dioxide is an essential element in the photosynthetic process. When the stomata close on a C_3 plant, the rate of photosynthesis drops drastically because of the blockage of carbon dioxide and can eventually stop altogether. This is why in the summer months, most plants turn brown and dry up during long periods without rain. C_4 plants, however, have the ability to use carbon dioxide very quickly and efficiently. This also allows C_4 plants to take in carbon dioxide at a much faster rate, since it is constantly being added to these 4-carbon chains. By being more efficient and better able to use carbon dioxide quickly, these plants can undergo photosynthesis in some of the most arid conditions. Scientists believe that the C_4 method of photosynthesis is an evolutionary step and that, over time, natural selection would cause more plants to develop similar methods of improving the efficiency of photosynthesis.

Another alternative pathway in plants is known as crassulacean acid metabolism, or CAM. The name refers to a type of plants because the scientists who discovered this alternate pathway in the 1940s first identified and studied it in plants from the family *crassulaceae*. Like most other members of the CAM plant group, *crassulaceae* plants live in hot, dry climates. Opening their stomata during the day would rob these plants of the water that is vital to continuing the photosynthetic process. Instead, CAM plants open their stomata at night when the cooler air slows the rate of evaporation. These plants take in carbon dioxide at night, but instead of using all of the carbon dioxide for photosynthesis right away, the plant stores the gas within its leaves by attaching it to an acid. When the Sun comes up and the temperatures rise, other plants are forced to open their stomata and lose their water in order to gain carbon dioxide; or, they slow down the rate of photosynthesis by closing their stomata and losing their source of carbon dioxide. That is when CAM plants use the carbon dioxide they have stored during the night to continue the photosynthetic process while their stomata remain closed. Pineapples are one example of a CAM plant that you may be familiar with. Like all CAM plants, pineapples have the ability to shut down their stomata during the day while they continue to make glucose using carbon dioxide stored during the night.

The plant cell has the ability to take sunlight, gas, and water and turn it into an energy source (sugar) that sustains the plant. Photosynthesis is essential to our lives, and we would not be able to survive if plants did not undergo this process. Plants provide the nutrients that heterotrophs (species that must find food and cannot make their own) need to exist. Plants also absorb carbon dioxide gas from the atmosphere and turn water into the oxygen that we breathe.

5

The Role of DNA and RNA in the Plant Cell

DNA—a nucleic acid that carries the genetic information in the cell—has become familiar to most people through television, books, news media, and school lessons. DNA can help us to better understand diseases, find killers, and discover information about our family history.

What purpose does DNA serve in cells? And why is it so essential for life? These are questions scientists began asking immediately following the discovery that the cell contained storehouses of genetic information within the nucleus.

As previously noted, DNA is essential for cells because it serves as a template for the production of proteins. These proteins are essential to the life of the cell; for example, they serve as the building blocks of cellular structures. The information for the construction of all proteins necessary to sustain the cell is stored within the DNA, and all of these proteins can be constructed by ribosomes on the endoplasmic reticulum (ER).

The process of DNA synthesis begins when the DNA's double helix, which looks very much like a twisted ladder, is opened up by an enzyme known as the helicase. This process of opening DNA with helicase is often referred to as "unzipping" DNA because the process is very similar in principle to unzipping a jacket or sweater. When you unzip a garment, the zipper slider separates the interlocking teeth. In a similar fashion, the helicase opens the DNA strands so that the information held within becomes available.

Once the DNA has been opened, it can be copied by the nucleic acid RNA. RNA stands for ribonucleic acid, and it is very similar to DNA except RNA has a slightly different structure than DNA. Also, RNA does

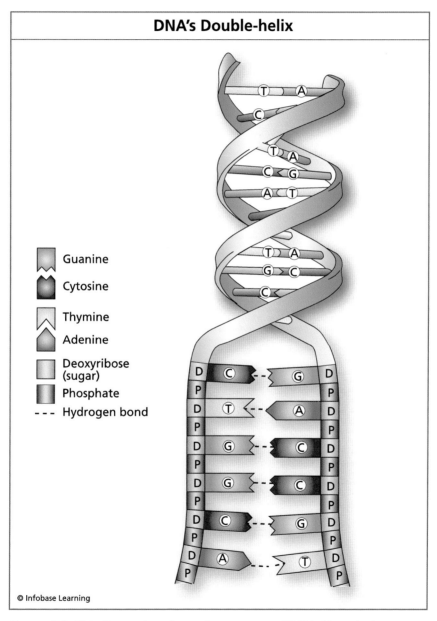

DNA's Double-helix

Guanine
Cytosine
Thymine
Adenine
Deoxyribose (sugar)
Phosphate
- - - Hydrogen bond

© Infobase Learning

FIGURE 5.1 This illustration shows the structure of DNA. Note the base pairs of nucleotides that make up the "rungs" of the ladder.

DNA Transcription

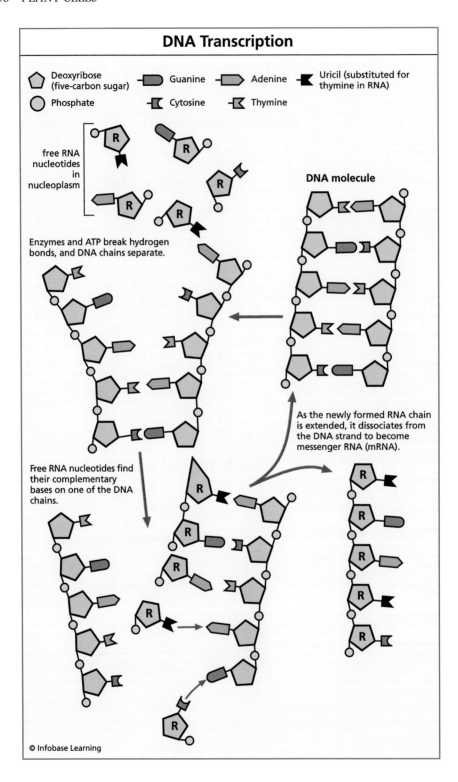

Deoxyribose (five-carbon sugar)

Phosphate

Guanine

Cytosine

Adenine

Thymine

Uricil (substituted for thymine in RNA)

free RNA nucleotides in nucleoplasm

DNA molecule

Enzymes and ATP break hydrogen bonds, and DNA chains separate.

As the newly formed RNA chain is extended, it dissociates from the DNA strand to become messenger RNA (mRNA).

Free RNA nucleotides find their complementary bases on one of the DNA chains.

(opposite page) FIGURE 5.2 DNA transcription is a process in which genetic information is transcribed from DNA to RNA.

not contain the same nucleotide bases as DNA. The rungs of DNA's double helix ladder are formed by the nucleotide bases. There are four nucleotide bases in DNA—adenine, guanine, cytosine, and thymine. Adenine bonds with thymine and cytosine bonds with guanine. These bonded pairs hold the two sides of DNA together.

When the helicase has exposed the inside by breaking these nucleotide bonds, a specific kind of RNA called mRNA can make copies of one side of the DNA strand. This is called transcription because the mRNA copies instructions down from the DNA. The mRNA reads and copies the DNA strand, in a fashion very similar to the other side of the DNA double helix strand that was "unzipped" by the helicase and taken away. The main difference is that the RNA does not contain the thymine base. Therefore, when the mRNA is copying the DNA sequence where a thymine would be located on a strand of DNA (across from adenine, which thymine bonds with) there is instead a different base called uracil. Other than the fact that RNA contains uracil instead of thymine, it is very similar to DNA.

When the transcription process is complete, the mRNA travels from the nucleus to the rough ER of the plant cell. As you may recall, the rough ER is where ribosomes build proteins. When the mRNA reaches the rough ER, it serves as a blueprint, using the information copied from the DNA to build proteins. Ribosomes use the codes taken from DNA in the nucleus to build amino acids, which are the building blocks of proteins.

Plants need proteins for a variety of reasons. We typically associate the term *protein* with nutrition. Meats like beef and chicken are sources of protein in our diet. However, plants rely on proteins, too. Proteins are everywhere in plants. They can even be found during a plant's embryonic stages. The molecules that capture light and allow for photosynthesis are made of proteins. Even the organelles are made of proteins, including the ribosomes that make other proteins.

Protein production is just one of the functions of the DNA in a plant. Cells, like all living things, have a lifespan. They live for a certain length of time and then they die. If these cells did not reproduce during that period, it would be impossible for plants to continue to grow.

For plant cells to reproduce, they must make a copy of themselves. This process of doubling DNA, where a single cell grows and separates into two

(continues on page 60)

BARBARA MCCLINTOCK
AND JUMPING GENES

Have you ever wondered why decorative corn has kernels of different colors on a single ear? Barbara McClintock, who spent most of her life studying heredity and genetic inheritance in plants, answered that question when she discovered a phenomenon she called transposition, also known as "jumping genes."

Barbara McClintock began her career as a plant geneticist when she enrolled at Cornell University in 1919. McClintock was immediately interested in genetics, a branch of science that was still relatively new and not well understood at that time. During her time at Cornell, McClintock was a standout student and her talents led her to research positions at various labs and universities, including the prestigious Cold Spring Harbor Laboratory. When she began to investigate the relationship of genes with cell characteristics, a science known as cytogenetics, she focused on a seemingly simple subject—maize, which we also know as corn. McClintock wanted to determine how genes in the chromosomes of corn affected things like height and color.

McClintock examined chromosomes of corn and realized that each gene had a specific location on a chromosome. During reproduction, genes "crossed over," resulting in offspring with varying sets of traits that are a unique combination of the genes of the parent plants. This is why only identical twin brother and sisters look exactly alike. McClintock discovered what she called transposons, which are also referred to as "jumping genes."

There were very few cytogeneticists during the 1930s. There were also very few women who were scientists. Barbara McClintock changed world views about genetics and the role of women in science. Her groundbreaking role as a woman studying high level, experimental genetics did as much to advance the role of female scientists as it did to increase our understanding of genetics.

Barbara McClintock was awarded the Nobel Prize in Science in 1983. She died in 1992 at the age of 90.

(opposite page) Figure 5.3 Barbara McClintock is pictured with the corn she was testing in Cold Spring Harbor Laboratory in 1947.

(continued from page 57)

cells, is known as **mitosis**. The process of mitosis occurs in both plant and animal cells, but the process is unique in plant cells because unlike animal cells, which have only a cell membrane, plants have cell walls. Plant growth requires that the cell wall be broken down so cell growth can take place. Then the cell wall has to be rebuilt. Because animal cells only have a cell membrane, they do not have to break down their cell walls during reproduction. The soft membranes on the outer portion of the cell simply pull apart. This characteristic is the biggest difference between plants and animal cell growth.

As in animal cells, plant cell mitosis is divided into five distinct stages. Sometimes these five stages are discussed as though they were equal parts of the plant cell life cycle, but this is not so. For most of the plant cell's life, it is simply undergoing the normal cellular processes. In short, it is simply being a cell and carrying out all of the normal functions of producing energy, removing wastes, and maintaining a stable environment within the cell. This longest phase of the plant cell's life is known as **interphase**. Although some of the first steps toward reproduction are occurring during this phase, the cell is still not undergoing actual cell division.

Because a plant's cells do not have the same intracellular network of fibers within them that the plant itself does, the first stage in mitosis is the movement of the nucleus to the center of the cell. This begins the first true step of the mitotic process known as **prophase**. The DNA within the cell has already replicated, and so there are two complete sets of DNA within the cells. These DNA strands are dark and highly visible under a microscope because, as the chromosomes prepare to split from one cell into two, the nuclear envelope surrounding the nucleus begins to break apart to allow the DNA to move into the new cells and form two new nuclei.

During the next step in the process of mitosis, the newly formed chromosome pairs line up in the middle of the cell in a process known as **metaphase**. During metaphase, all of the chromosomes that have doubled are neatly arranged and aligned on the central axis of the cell in preparation for the next step in the process. If you examine plant cells with a compound light microscope while they are undergoing mitosis, it is very easy to distinguish cells that are in metaphase because all of the paired chromosomes are lined up in the center of the cell and appear as a series of "x"s as they await separation.

Following metaphase, the doubled chromosomes begin to split and pull toward opposite sides of the cell. This step of mitosis is known as

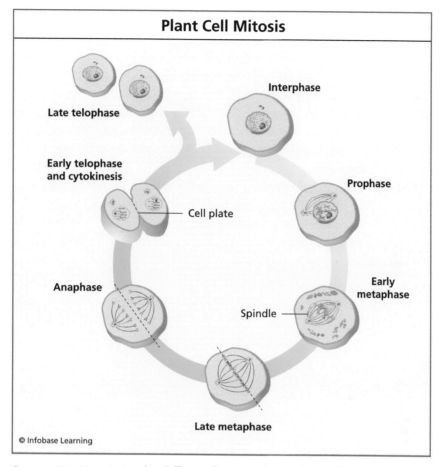

FIGURE 5.4 Mitosis is a bit different for animal and plant cells because these kinds of cells are structured differently. For example, animal cells have centrioles, while plant cells do not. Also, plant cells have a cell wall, while animal cells do not. The major difference between plant and animal cell mitosis is that during the plant cell's final phase, a cell plate forms across the middle of it, dividing the cell in two.

anaphase. Because the cell has two complete sets of chromosomes after replication in interphase, the chromosome sets that pull apart are two sets identical to the original set of chromosomes that were in the plant's nucleus when the entire process began. In anaphase, the chromosomes move away from midline and begin to form two new **daughter cells**. These daughter cells will be exactly alike, providing that nothing has gone wrong during the chromosome replication process.

In animal cells, the cell membranes begin to pinch in during ana-phase and form what scientists call a cleavage furrow. Plants have cell walls, however, that cannot easily be pinched in since they are rigid. This is not a problem for the cells, though. During the final stage of mitosis, which is known as **telophase**, the Golgi apparatus begins to form a wall that separates the two daughter cells. This cell plate will form the new cell wall between the daughter cells. During telophase, the chromosomes lighten and unwind, and the daughter cells continue the processes of life as cells in interphase.

Mitosis can occur throughout the plant, but in some areas of the plant, it occurs more often. The tip of the main roots, for instance, is where the plant needs to continue to grow very quickly so it can reach deeper into the ground. Mitosis also occurs frequently near the end of limbs where leaf buds appear in the spring.

6

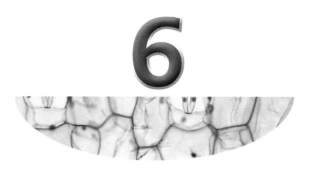

Plant Reproduction

When a nineteenth-century Austrian monk named Gregor Mendel crossed pea plants with purple flowers with pea plants that had white flowers, he was shocked by what he found. The offspring of the cross between purple flowering peas and white flowering peas produced offspring that only had purple flowers. Furthermore, no matter how many times he crossed the peas, the same result occurred every time.

Adding to Mendel's confusion was the fact that when he crossed two purple flowers from the second generation of his experiment, the plants produced sometimes had white flowers. From that point, Mendel set out to discover the reason for this seemingly counterintuitive trait in pea plants. Why did crossing a purple and white flower always produce purple flowers and crossing the resulting two purple flowers sometimes produce a white flowering pea plant?

Mendel spent years working with peas in the garden of the monastery where he lived in Austria. After making several thousand crosses with pea plants, he realized that there were some constants in the coloring of offspring from his pea plant crosses. Mendel proposed the idea that plants passed on their genetic material, and that the genetic material passed down from both parent plants controlled several factors in the offspring, including the color of the flower.

Gregor Mendel is known today as the father of the study of genetics. Genetics is the science that examines traits that are carried in genetic material and how those traits affect offspring. All of the traits in a plant—

how tall it grows, how it undergoes photosynthesis, how it reproduces, and its color—are all determined by the DNA passed down from the parent plants.

Plants are similar to animals in the fact that every characteristic of the plant's physical makeup is determined by information coded in DNA in genes. Furthermore, the genes of a plant or animal are a random combination of characteristics from both parents.

The first step of plant reproduction involves cells. These plant cells, called sex cells, are produced through a process called meiosis. We must not confuse meiosis with mitosis. In mitosis, a cell makes a duplicate copy of its DNA and divides into two daughter cells that have the exact same characteristics. Meiosis, however, produces sex cells that normally contain half of the parent plant's DNA. Because sexual reproduction results in the combining of DNA from both parent plants, each parent produces sex cells that contain only a portion of that plant's total DNA. The resulting embryo, therefore, contains DNA from both of the parent plants. However, the combination of these two sets of DNA makes the offspring a unique combination of both parent plants.

Before meiosis begins, the cell goes through interphase just as it does in mitosis. In meiosis, the interphase stage is divided into two distinct periods known as Gap 1 (G1) and Synthesis (S). The G1 phase is a period of rapid growth within the cell. The S phase is the period when the plant cell actually makes a copy of its DNA. This DNA copy will help carry the genes of the parent plant to the offspring when fertilization occurs. Much like it does in the parent plant, the DNA that is passed down from parent to offspring will act as a blueprint for the production of proteins within the offspring.

Meiosis is divided into two stages known as meiosis I and meiosis II. At first glance, the steps in meiosis appear to be very similar to the steps in mitosis and, in fact, the general stages and many events do resemble mitosis. The end result of meiosis, however, is very different. Whereas one complete cycle of mitosis produces two identical daughter cells, one cycle of meiosis produces four haploid sex cells that contain half the parent plant's DNA. These haploid plant cells have only half of the parent plant's DNA, so that they can recombine with another haploid cell during reproduction.

Meiosis begins with the onset of prophase I, which is identical to prophase I in mitosis. During this stage, the chromosomes darken much like they do in mitotic division. Chromosomal DNA is mixed in a process called recombination. During recombination, chromosomes "cross over" and new chromosomal patterns develop. This prevents offspring from having the same genetic code as the parent plant.

In metaphase I, the second stage of meiosis, the newly recombined chromosomes line up along the middle of the cell and the darkened, paired chromosomes become clearly visible as they are during the same stage in mitosis. These paired chromosomes line up along the equatorial region of the cell (the middle) and wait to be separated. Spindle fibers, which work like ropes attached to a stage curtain, appear within the cell. In the next stage, the spindle fibers separate the chromosomes.

Separation of the chromosomes initially occurs during anaphase I of cellular meiosis. The identical chromosome pairs, which were copied during the S phase of interphase, are known as **homologous pairs**. Homologous chromosomes are chromosomes that are identical. These homologous chromosomes begin to separate during anaphase I. The spindle fibers that appeared in metaphase I begin to separate the chromosomes and direct the homologous pairs toward opposite poles of the plant cell.

At the end of anaphase I, the new cell plate is formed by proteins, and the chromosomes appear in two separate cells. The cell wall becomes apparent in telophase I, which is the last step in meiosis I. Up until this point, the processes of meiosis have been very similar to the steps of mitosis. Unlike mitosis, though, the process of meiosis is only halfway complete. Meiosis includes a second cycle that begins at the end of telophase I. The daughter cells, which are diploid (containing a full set of chromosomes), must divide again. This begins the second half of the process of meiosis which is known as meiosis II.

The first stage in meiosis II is prophase II. The $2n$ daughter cells darken and remain visible as the newly constructed cell wall finishes assembling. Inside of their new cell walls, both daughter cells once again line up along the equator of their respective cells, once more held in place by spindle fibers. At first glance, meiosis II appears very much like meiosis I, but there are some subtle differences that can be detected by trained cell biologists. For one thing, the two daughter cells are going through the exact same process at the exact same time in cells that are right next to one another. In addition, because they have divided, there are only half of the chromosomes present in meiosis II as there are in meiosis I.

By the time the cell reaches anaphase II, meiosis is nearly complete. Spindle fibers pull the **chromatids**, which are bundles of chromosomes, apart. The chromatids then move away from the equator of the cell toward their respective poles.

The final stage in meiosis is telophase II. By now, the spindle fibers have directed the chromatids to opposite poles in the newly developed plant cells. Proteins begin to assemble to form two new cell walls are that are perpendicular to the cell wall developed in telophase I of meiosis. In telophase II, the chromatids are covered by a newly formed nuclear envelope and disappear from view. The entire process of meiosis is complete and the end result is four daughter cells that are haploid, or *n*, and which contain only half of the genetic material of the parent cell.

Most of the cells in a plant contain a set of DNA from both of the parent plants. These cells are called diploid cells and are represented as *2n*. However, the reproductive cells in plants, which are called haploid cells and are represented by *n*, contain only half of a complete set of chromosomes. When the sex cells from the male portion of the plant fertilize the female sex cells, the resulting embryos receive the haploid (*n*) cells from the male plant and the haploid (*n*) cells from the female plant. The result is a unique diploid (*2n*) offspring.

Plants do not always follow the same pattern as animals in regard to their diploid count. In humans, all the cells, except sex cells, are diploid (*2n*). When meiosis occurs, haploid sex cells are formed. During fertilization, the haploid sex cells from a man and a woman combine to form a diploid cell that will develop into an embryo and, ultimately, a mature diploid human being. However, certain plants, such as ferns, do not follow this pattern. When ferns are ready to reproduce, spores develop on the underside of the leaf. These spores are called **sori** and are oftentimes visible if you look at the bottom of a fern leaf. When sori reach maturity, they drop from the adult fern and usually settle near the adult plant. The individual spore then puts down thin roots known as rhizomes and begins to develop into what appears to be a small plant that is known as a **gametophyte**. Gametophytes remain in a haploid (*n*) state until fertilization occurs. This happens when sperm from a mature plant swims to the gametophyte, an action that only occurs when there is significant moisture. (This is the reason why ferns are found in damp, shaded forests.) When the sperm reaches the gametophyte, the gametophyte is fertilized and turns into the diploid (*2n*) version of a fern that we all recognize. This diploid version of the plant is known as the **sporophyte** version. This cycle of diploid and haploid reproduction is known as **alternation of generations**. Alternation of generation occurs in all plants but, unlike humans, not all plants are initially diploid during their first stages of life.

Plants do not always follow this same pattern, however. Many plants contain more than two sets of DNA. These plants are referred to as polyploid plants. Polyploid plants contain more—sometimes many more—than two sets of DNA. Polyploidy is sometimes the result of a mistake that occurs during meiosis. Some sex cells in plants contain two sets of DNA instead of one and are therefore diploid instead of haploid. The result is an offspring that contains three sets of DNA. Such a plant is referred to as a triploid and is represented by 3*n*. These mistakes are not always bad. Polyploidy can actually help plants to survive better by producing larger flowers with more petals and larger fruit. In fact, some agricultural plants are intentionally bred to exhibit polyploidy because polyploidy plants are sometimes better suited to the environment and produce larger fruit. Many domestic plants, such as roses, are bred from polyploidy strains to produce variations in flower color and an increase in the size and petal count of flowers. Scientists have manipulated polyploidy plants so that they can control the additional genes present. Some examples of this manipulation are domesticated corn and store-bought flowers. The next time that you see a rose, remember that the wild ancestor of that flower had five small petals.

REPRODUCTION IN PLANTS WITH SEEDS

Ferns and mosses require water for reproduction. However, if all plants required wet conditions for reproduction and survival, then only the wettest places on Earth would have plants. This is not the case, however. Plants are found around the globe, from the hottest deserts to the driest arctic tundra. For survival in such harsh conditions, plants had to adapt methods to reproduce that did not require constant water. One of the greatest adaptations in plants was the development of seeds. **Seeds** are structures that are designed to protect the developing embryo, or **zygote**, from conditions that could prevent it from successfully developing into an adult plant. Seeds protect the embryo from the threat of **desiccation**, or drying out. Seeds also allow the plant embryo to lie dormant for weeks, months, or even longer in some cases. The seed coat, or husk, is the protective coating that surrounds the embryo and the starch that feeds the embryo while it is still within the seed coat.

Reproduction in seed-bearing plants does not require water like the reproductive processes of mosses and ferns do. Plants produce pollen grains that contain sperm. For reproduction to occur, this single-celled sperm inside the pollen grain must somehow reach the pistil, or female portion, of the plant. Pollen grains protect the sperm and allow it to travel to the anther, a journey that sometimes takes a long time over a large distance without drying out the way that fern sperm would if there were no water.

There are a wide variety of ways that the sperm in a grain of pollen can reach the pistil. One of these methods is by wind. Certain plants produce huge amounts of pollen that are light enough to be blown on wind currents toward other plants of the same species. These plants oftentimes

LESSONS FROM THE DUST BOWL

Early nineteenth-century settlers found a land with great potential when they settled in America's Great Plains region, which includes Kansas, Oklahoma, and Nebraska. The plains were covered with grasses that fed great herds of wild game, including bison, pronghorn antelope, and deer. In an effort to turn maximum profit from these areas, settlers killed off most of the native game species and replaced them with great herds of cattle that overgrazed the grass. In addition, farmers plowed the ground and killed many native plants and planted corn, wheat, and vegetables in their place.

What these early settlers didn't know, however, was that the plants that lived on the prairie were specially adapted to survive on the harsh plains during periods of drought and high wind. Their root systems had evolved to form a network that also held the soil in place against the combination of dry conditions and high winds that threatened the soil.

The crops that farmers planted, however, did not have the same root adaptations as the native plants. Meanwhile, a combination of the hooves of the great cattle herds and rampant overgrazing left the plains largely devoid of the native grasses that once protected it. When drought and windstorms swept across the plains in the 1920s and 1930s, the fragile soil turned to dust and drove many settlers away. Great clouds of dust, lifted up into the sky by high winds, buried homes and abandoned settlements. The bounty of the plains had been depleted, and all that remained was a dry, desolate landscape where neither man nor animal could survive.

do not have brightly colored flowers because they do not have to attract pollinators like bees and birds. Since they reproduce by flooding the air with pollen, they are also among the most irritating plants to allergy sufferers. Plants that spread their pollen through the wind are known as **anemochoric** plants. Ragweed is a common example of an anemochoric plant and one that causes a great deal of suffering for people with allergies as it releases huge amounts of pollen in the fall of the year. Other anemochoric plants include grasses and many of the coniferous, or cone bearing, plants.

In response to the Dust Bowl, the government established the Soil Conservation service in 1935 to prevent such disasters from occurring again. Today, programs to reintroduce native grasses and farming that utilizes no-till planting procedures have greatly reduced the risk of another dust bowl anytime in the near future.

Figure 6.1 A dried-out farm near Dalhart, Texas, is pictured during the Dust Bowl in the 1930s. Although a family lived in this home, most of the houses in this district were abandoned due to the difficult living conditions that included severe dust storms and drought.

Other plants spread their pollen with the help of animals. Some plant species have beautiful flowers that attract pollinators, such as birds, flies, beetles, and bees, as well as other insects that likely visit several plants. Animals that carry pollen from one plant to the next are known as **pollinators**. As these pollinators move from one plant to the next in search of a meal, they inadvertently carry pollen along with them, assisting in the process of pollination and reproduction. Plants that reproduce with the help of animal pollinators are known as **zoochoric** plants.

Some plants have the ability to pollinate themselves. However, these plants sometimes still require a pollinator to spread the pollen to the **ovule**, or female reproductive cell, of the plant. Some plants can fertilize the ovule of one flower with the pollen of that same flower and others require that the pollen comes from a different flower. Sometimes cross-pollination can occur between very closely related species, which results in a **hybrid** plant that contains genes from both species. However, this only occurs in plants that are closely related. Rose pollen, for example, cannot fertilize a plant from the violet family.

Are plants male, female, or both? That depends upon the plant. Some plants have both male and female portions (pollen and ovules) on the same plant. Sometimes these male and female portions of the plant are located together and sometimes they are found in separate locations. Plants that have both male and female components in the same plant are known as **monoecious** plants. All monoecious plants have both female and male reproductive parts and, therefore, they are both male and female. Other plants, like ginkgo trees, are either male or female and do not have both male and female reproductive structures in the same plant. For reproduction to occur, both male and female plants must grow in the same vicinity. Plants that are either male or female are known as **dioecious** plants.

Seed-producing plants are divided into two dominant groups. One of these groups, the **gymnosperms**, contains many of the world's most ancient plant species. Gymnosperms include all of the cone-bearing plants such as pine trees, as well as cycads and ginkgoes. Like all seed bearing plants, the gymnosperms produce pollen that must be released to come in contact with the ovule of the plant. Most gymnosperms are anemochoric. The term gymnosperm is a combination of the root words *gymno*, which

---

(opposite page) FIGURE 6.2 Pollination is the transfer of pollen from a male anther to a female carpel. This is usually carried out with the help of insects and the wind.

Types of Pollination

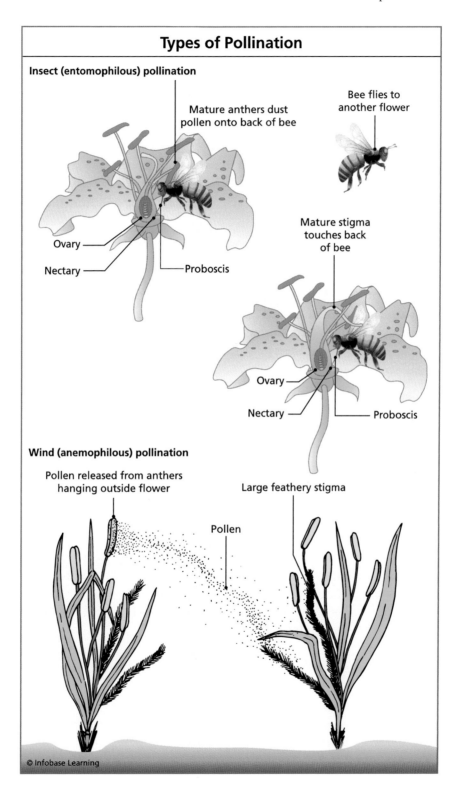

Insect (entomophilous) pollination

Mature anthers dust pollen onto back of bee

Bee flies to another flower

Ovary

Nectary

Proboscis

Mature stigma touches back of bee

Ovary

Nectary

Proboscis

Wind (anemophilous) pollination

Pollen released from anthers hanging outside flower

Large feathery stigma

Pollen

© Infobase Learning

means "naked," and *sperm*, which means "seed," and they are, therefore, referred to as "naked seeds." They differ from traditional flowering plants in that the fertilized embryo, while it remains in a seed coat, develops on the scales of a cone and is not separated from the environment as it is with flowering plants.

Most of the gymnosperms on the planet today are in the division Coniferophyta and are known as conifers, or cone-bearing plants. Conifers are also commonly called pine trees or evergreens. They are called evergreens because many of the members of division Coniferophyta do not appear to lose their leaves, which are usually long and thin and are referred to as needles. In actuality, conifers shed their needles periodically but the continual regeneration of needles makes it appear as though the plant never loses it leaves, even in winter. They are, in fact, gradually replaced over time.

Pines, firs, cedars, and spruce trees are all common examples of coniferous trees found in the United States. The massive red sequoias, the largest and oldest living organisms on the planet, are conifers. It may be hard to imagine, but these ancient trees, many of which are as tall as skyscrapers, all started out as small cones.

Conifers have separate male and female cones that can oftentimes be seen on the same plant. The male portion, called a pollen cone, is generally smaller and less noticeable than the female seed cone. Pollen cones are oftentimes higher on the tree and are not hard and scaly like seed cones. Pollen cones release huge amounts of pollen that drift down on air currents toward the female seed cone. The seed cone produces a sticky substance that is designed to catch any falling pollen so that the ovule of the seed cone can be fertilized. If the pollen reaches the ovule on the seed and fertilizes the ovule, the cone drops to the ground and, if conditions are good, a new conifer begins to grow. Sometimes in the spring, large amounts of pollen particles can be seen on the surface of water or on roads near pine trees.

Conifers make up only a small portion of the plants in the world today. Most plants are classified as **angiosperms**. Angiosperms represent the latest stage in the evolution of plant reproduction. They have developed a unique reproductive structure that has helped them to evolve into the most successful plants on Earth. This special structure is noted for its beauty and fine fragrance, but is not often thought of as one of the greatest evolutionary developments in plants. These unique structures are flowers. Angiosperms are more commonly called flowering plants.

Flowers come in a wide variety of shapes, colors, and sizes. The cells of a flower are among the most specialized in all plant species. Flowers contain both the male and female portions of the plant and the petals of a flower all contain highly specialized cells that cooperate to complete one task—reproduction.

Most plants have monoecious flowers. Both the male and female portion of the plant exist on the same flower and serve separate functions that are essential to reproduction. Both the male and female portions of the flower produce gametophytes for reproduction. The male portion of the flower is known as the **stamen**. Flowers usually have several stamens that rise up from the center of the petals in a ring that surrounds the female portion of the plant, which is known as the **pistil**. The stamens of male plants have long, thin filaments that elevate the pollen-producing **anthers** high into the air. The anthers, which are usually oval shaped, contain thousands of pollen grains. Each pollen grain has the potential to fertilize

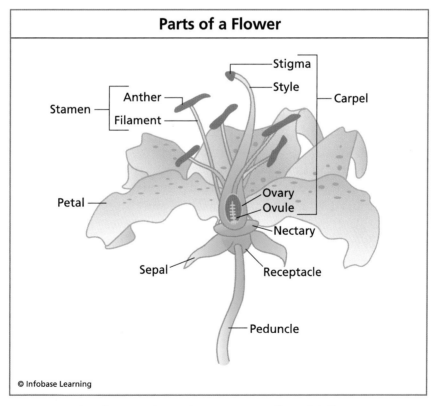

Parts of a Flower

Stigma

Style

Carpel

Anther

Stamen

Filament

Petal

Ovary

Ovule

Nectary

Sepal

Receptacle

Peduncle

© Infobase Learning

FIGURE 6.3 This diagram shows the main parts of an adult flower.

another flower (or, in some cases, the same flower). However, in order for their pollen grains to be spread, zoochoric plants rely on bees, flies, birds, or other animals to carry their pollen to the pistil.

The pistil is the female portion of the flower. It usually lies at the center and contains four essential components: stigma, style, ovules, and the ovary. The **stigma** is the most superior (or highest) portion of the pistil. Pollen grains are captured by the stigma and move down the tube below. This tube is known as the **style**, and it serves to direct the growth of pollen tubes that grow from the pollen grain to the ovule, where fertilization occurs. The style is the tube that serves as a connector for the pollen grain and the ovule. The ovules are kept within the **ovary** of the plant. It is within the ovary that fertilization occurs, and the new plant embryo begins to develop. The specialized cells within the flower assist the plant in reproduction and soon the growing embryo begins the processes of growth and cellular reproduction within the confines of a protective outer coating.

FROM THE GROUND UP: EMBRYO DEVELOPMENT

Have you ever eaten a peanut? Odds are that you have, but what you probably haven't done is examine the peanut before you ate it. If you did, you would notice that located between the two halves of the peanut is a pointed piece, which is actually a fertilized embryo that would have developed into a peanut plant.

Why does such a small embryo require a whole peanut for its development? What purpose do all the additional portions of the peanut serve in the growth and development of the small embryo?

While plants do not tend to their offspring in the way that mammals do, they do go to their own extremes to be sure that their offspring have a good chance of survival. Plants begin preparing for their offspring during fertilization. A pollen grain actually contains two nuclei. Only one of these sperm nuclei fertilizes the waiting ovule. The other nucleus develops into a carbohydrate that will feed the embryo as it develops (peanuts, like other seeds, are therefore 3*n* or triploid with 3 sets of DNA). This process of fertilization with two sperm where one develops into a food source while the other fertilizes the ovule is referred to by scientists as double fertilization. This rich carbohydrate, which is called **endosperm**, provides all the nutrients needed by the growing embryo. In fact, most of the food eaten by humans around the world is made up of the endosperm of plants.

Corn, wheat, nuts, and rice grains are all composed primarily of endosperm. The endosperm of plant cells is often referred to as starch.

Endosperms in plant cells are unique in that they do not form unless the plant is fertilized. Since the flower requires a pollen grain to undergo the fertilization and to form the endosperm, no endosperm will be formed in an unfertilized flower. This prevents the plant from wasting the energy necessary to develop an endosperm if fertilization has not occurred. By conserving this energy, plant cells have more resources available to undergo other processes like food production and the production of chemical defenses.

Once the ovule is fertilized, the process of fruit development begins. **Fruits** are the thickened walls of ovaries that contain the fertilized seeds and that protect and nourish the seed. This includes foods that we traditionally view as fruits like apples and oranges, as well as other foods like peas, beans and cucumbers: All of these contain fertilized seeds within a protective coating. After fertilization has occurred, the single-celled embryo begins to undergo mitotic division, doubling and doubling again as it grows and develops within the confines of the seed. Meanwhile, the cells of the plant ovary begin to thicken into the walls of the fruit. These thickened walls serve several purposes that benefit the developing embryo within the seed. Fruits protect the seed from desiccation by surrounding the seed with a waxy layer that prevents water loss. This wax layer, which is seen on the surface of fruits like apples, also protects the seeds from infection and disease by forming a waterproof barrier.

Fruits are a favorite food for birds and animals alike. It may seem odd that the plant *wants* the seeds it has produced to be eaten by animals, but oftentimes that is exactly how a new plant is made to grow in a different location where it will not interfere or compete with the parent plant. Berries, which are a form of fruit, are often eaten by birds that later fly to different locations where the seeds inside the fruit are deposited with the bird waste. This aids the plant in the dispersal of seeds and helps plant species spread to new areas.

The endosperm in angiosperms develops in one of two ways. Some plant species, like peanuts, develop an endosperm that contains two halves. These plants are referred to as **dicotyledons** or, more simply, dicots. Peanuts and beans are examples of dicots. If you have ever eaten peanuts, you have probably noticed that the endosperm of the peanut often breaks into two halves. Other plants, like corns and grasses, have one solid endosperm that feeds the embryo. These plants are referred to as **monocotyledons,** or

THE LAND OF GIANTS
. . . .

Northern California and southern Oregon are home to the world's tallest trees, *Sequoia sempervirens*. Today, these trees are better known as redwoods, a coniferous species that grows to incredible heights, some as high as a 40-story skyscraper. These trees live an average of 500 to 700 years but may live as long as 2,000 years. This means that the same trees that live on the western coast of the United States were there during the time of the Roman Empire, the Dark Ages, and had fully matured when Christopher Columbus and other European explorers first landed in the western hemisphere.

Redwoods get their name from the reddish brown color of their wood, which is covered with an outer layer of gray shaggy bark. The most famous redwoods can be found along the Avenue of Giants on the California coast. Each year, thousands of people make the trip to see these miraculous organisms that tower hundreds of feet above the ground. There are even redwoods that are large enough to allow cars to drive through their massive trunks. Despite their great size, the redwoods all began their lives as a single plant cell, perhaps as many as 2,000 years ago.

monocots. Scientists use these two endosperm varieties to divide angiosperms into two separate classes.

Monocots and dicots vary in other ways as well. The monocot class of plants has leaves with parallel veins. If you examine blades of grass or corn stalks, you will find that all of the veins in their leaves run in the same direction along the length of their stems. Dicots have veins that branch and do not run in the same direction. Many trees like oaks and maples have branching veins in their leaves, which is a sure sign they are dicots. Another difference between the two classes is in their roots. Monocots have roots that spread in all directions from their point of origin. These types of roots are known as *fibrous roots*. If you pull a clump of grass from the ground, you will see that the roots go in all directions. Dicots, on the other hand, have one, large, main root that smaller roots branch off of. This main root, known as the **taproot**, makes up the bulk of the mass of the roots, and it typically grows straight down. Carrots are an example of a dicot with a taproot.

Both monocots and dicots do have one thing in common—for their embryos to grow into healthy adult plants, they must land in a suitable location and they must germinate. **Germination** is the process where the embryonic plant bursts through the seed coat and begins the process of independent food production. Germination requires water. The water is absorbed by the immature plant cells inside the seed, which fill up, expanding in size until the seed coat finally bursts and the new plant emerges. Cells in the plant then begin to specialize. Some cells dive into the soil and grow downward. These cells form what is known as the **radicle,** or the initial root. Cells that develop into the radicle are not green because they are underground away from sunlight and, therefore, do not participate in photosynthesis. Other cells begin to specialize to form the portion of the plant that is visible above ground. The stem and leaves turn green as chlorophyll is produced and the plant begins the process of photosynthesis.

Some seeds do not immediately germinate. Sometimes, conditions are not favorable for plant growth and the seedling, or baby plant, does not survive. In many cases, plants have the ability to go through a period of dormancy. Dormancy is a period in the plant's life when germination is stalled because of unfavorable conditions. Dormant seeds can remain viable for long periods of time, outlasting snowy winters, hot summers, drought, and even forest fires, so that they can germinate when the conditions are favorable. Dormant plants can sometimes go years before the new plant germinates.

Germination represents the final step in the process of an embryo developing into a seedling plant that is capable of surviving on its own. However, the seedling requires a great deal of cooperation from a variety of different cells types that work together so that the plant will survive and pass on its genes to future generations.

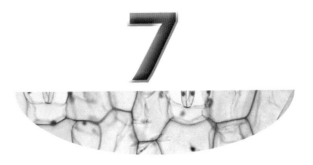

7

Specialized
Plant Cells

After germination, plant cells begin to grow and divide rapidly. All of the necessary information for producing proteins and for the formation of specialized plant cells is held within the DNA of the seedling plant. As the seedling begins to grow, the cells begin to specialize into different cells with unique structures and functions that are designed to help the plant survive and reproduce.

Plant cells come in a wide variety to help increase the plant's chances of survival. Immediately after germination occurs, the seedling is already producing cells that look very different and that will serve independent roles to insure that the plant has the ability to thrive in its new world. Some plant cells specialize in anchoring the plant against harsh winds. Other cells help carry water and nutrients throughout the plant while other cells work to produce food through photosynthesis. Still others focus on the task of protecting the plant from insects and herbivores that might eat it. All of these cells work as a coordinated team.

Plants may seem inactive and lifeless, but this is not the case. From the moment a plant germinates, a flurry of activity occurs within the plant: Water and nutrients are moved up and down the stem; chloroplasts are constantly working to pump out the sugar that feeds the plant; pollen and ovules are being produced for reproduction. During this entire process, cells are multiplying while the plant grows from a seedling into an adult. None of this would be possible were it not for the continuous work of plant cells. In reality, a plant is a living, breathing

SOCRATES'S UNFORTUNATE END

Greek philosopher Socrates was best known for his development of social and moral ideals that led to the ideas of democratic rule. His student Plato, another Greek philosopher, wrote about Socrates' ideas and principles, which were not widely accepted in Athens at the time. Although Socrates' idea that everyone should have equal say in how government is run is a principle that is widely accepted in many countries today, at the time Socrates lived (469 B.C.–399 B.C.) Greek society was ruled by only a chosen few. Socrates disagreed with this principle and challenged Athenian rule. As a result, he was sentenced to death and ordered to drink a poison derived from the root of a plant in the hemlock family.

Hemlock plants belong to the family *Apiaceae*. There are a variety of hemlock plants that live around the world. Poison hemlock, the variety of hemlock that was ground up and used to kill Socrates, is found in Europe near the Mediterranean Sea. Other varieties of hemlock are found

throughout the world. One of these varieties, which has white flower clusters that grow on long, thin, upright stems is known as Queen Anne's lace. The compound flowers, when bunched together, somewhat resemble lace. Considered to be a weed and a pest in agricultural areas, Queen Anne's lace is actually very closely

(continues)

Figure 7.1 Queen Anne's lace is believed to help with tomato and lettuce plant production. When grown in large patches, it increases the cool, moist air that optimizes growing conditions for these vegetables.

(continued)

related to the domestic carrot. However, the root of Queen Anne's lace, unlike the more common carrot that we eat, is not normally used as a food source because the roots are much more fibrous and woodlike in the adult plant. Still, when we eat a carrot, we are eating a plant that is very closely related to the plant that killed Socrates more than 2,000 years ago in Greece.

organism that is constantly reacting to outside stimulation and environmental changes.

Groups of cells with similar form and function create **tissues**. There are a variety of tissues in plants. Much as tissues do in our own bodies, these tissues work together to form **organs**. Organs are the organized units within the plant that are responsible for life processes. Organs are all made up of great numbers of cells. Leaves, roots, and stems are all plant organs.

PLANT TISSUES

Plants contain three varieties of tissues: dermal, vascular, and ground tissue. All three tissues are comprised of cells with unique characteristics that help them perform the functions necessary for the survival of the plant. **Dermal plant tissues** protect the plant from the outside environment. Dermal tissues in plants act in much the same way that our skin works. On the outer surface of the dermal tissue is a layer of specialized cells known as epidermal cells (*epi* is the Greek for "upon," and *derm* is the Greek for "skin"). These cells have thick walls and act together in coordination to protect other plant tissues from damage. Epidermal cells are among the toughest cells within the plant and they are also oftentimes coated in a waxy film that helps protect the plant from disease and infection. This waxy layer on top of the epidermis of plant cells is known as the **cuticle**. Beneath the epidermis lies the dermal layer. Dermal tissue occurs throughout the plant and many dermal cells are specialized to perform a specific task.

Dermal cells are some of the most specialized cells in a plant. Dermal cells have the responsibility to protect the plant from insects and herbivores that would eat it. Several plant species have dermal cells that are specialized to keep animals from eating the leaves and stems. One example of a protective adaptation in a plant's dermal cells are prickles. **Prickles** are extensions of the plant that have a sharp point like those found on flowers like roses. Prickles are similar in form to two other plant defenses:

FIGURE 7.2 Thorns cover this Chinese honey locust tree.

thorns and spines. **Thorns** are modified portions of the plant stem, and **spines** are modified leaves. Thorns often branch out and can be found on trees such as the honey locust and acacia, while spines are often shorter and do not branch. Cacti, for example, have spines.

Another dermal adaptation that acts to protect the plant is trichomes. Trichomes are small hairs that grow over the surface of some species of plants, particularly on the stems and leaves. These specialized hairs on the epidermis protect the plant in a variety of ways. Some trichomes irritate herbivores and reduce the chances of a plant being eaten. Trichomes may also serve to reduce the loss of water through evaporation and keep water from gathering in pools on leaves and stems, which can lead to fungal infections.

Dermal cells also control the amount of water going into and out of a plant's leaves. As noted previously, plants require CO_2 to undergo photosynthesis. This gas comes from the air and is collected through openings on the underside of the leaf called guard cells that open and close as needed. Many plants have cells that can expand and contract so that guard cells can open during the cooler periods of the day and can completely close during the hotter times of the day.

Beneath the plant's dermal tissue layer lies the **ground tissue**. This tissue lies between the dermal tissue and the inner vascular tissue in plants and serves a wide variety of functions. Ground tissue makes up the cortex of the plant, a region that separates the outer portion of the stem from the interior portion. This cortex wall oftentimes contains large cells that serve to store nutrients for the plant.

Ground tissue is divided into three separate categories. The most common variety is **parenchyma**, which are thin-walled cells, each of which has large openings. Other ground tissue cells are classified as **collenchyma** cells. Like parenchyma cells, collenchyma cells have large amounts of fluid-filled space within them, but unlike parenchyma cells, they are flexible and have thickened cell walls capable of withstanding large amounts of strain. The third variety of ground tissue is known as **sclerenchyma**, which is made of cells that have little fluid inside of them and have very rigid cell walls that provide the plant cell with support. Sclerenchyma cells provide the framework inside a large plant or tree that prevents them from breaking and falling down when they are under great strain.

The last type of plant tissue is one of the most essential because it allows for the movement of fluids and sugars throughout the plant. This tissue is known as vascular tissue. **Vascular tissue** in plants serves like our

Inside Tree and Plant Stems

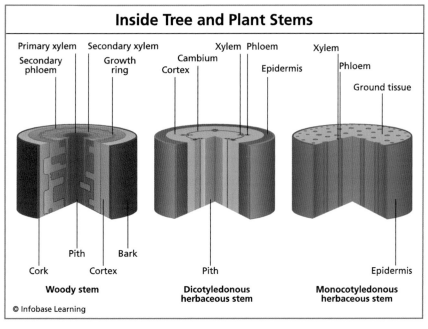

FIGURE 7.3 A stem provides support and a pathway for fluid transport.

own vascular system, moving materials wherever they are needed through a system of channels that run throughout the organism.

Vascular tissues in plants are divided into two main categories: **xylem** and **phloem**. Xylem and phloem are similar in that they are both tubes that carry materials throughout the plant, but they differ in a variety of ways. Xylem transports water through a series of specialized cells called tracheids. As the plant grows, tracheid cells stack up on top of each other and dry out to become long waterproof tubes that are perfect for carrying water throughout the plant. In very large plants, such as the giant sequoia trees of northern California, xylem carries water up tubes that are several stories high—higher than most elevators can reach. How is that plants are able to move water up through their stems?

The walls of xylem cells contain large amounts of cellulose. The cellulose forms a matrix that water molecules cling to. Through a process called **capillary action**, water is drawn from the roots of the plant up the xylem to the leaves, branches, flowers, and every other portion of the tree or plant. (Capillary action is the movement of water upward in a tube because of the cohesive, or self-bonding, properties of water.) As water vapor is lost through evaporation, a process called **transpiration**, more water is pulled up the xylem tubes from the roots below. Roots continue to pull water in from the ground and this water is continuously pulled upward through all the plant's tissues. The combination of these three factors (capillary action, transpiration, and root pressure) enables the tallest plants and trees to transport water and nutrients up through the xylem. This is the result of many specialized cells working together in coordination.

Phloem is another specialized tissue in plants that works to transport materials through vascular tubes. Phloem is a collection of highly specialized cells, which are called **sieve tube elements,** and **companion cells** that combine together in tubes that transport nutrients within the plant. Sieve

PLANTS IN CRIME

One of the most famous kidnappings and murders in American history is that of Charles Lindbergh Jr, the child of aviator Charles Lindbergh. At the time this crime was committed, in the 1930s, very little was known about forensics and very few criminal cases involved forensic evidence. In a groundbreaking decision, the judge in the Lindbergh trial allowed Dr. Arthur Koehler, an expert in wood and wood fibers, to testify regarding a ladder that was alleged to have been used in the kidnapping. Bruno Hauptmann, the main suspect, had supposedly used the ladder to climb into the Lindbergh house and kidnap the child.

The courtroom was fascinated by Dr. Koehler's testimony. Koehler testified that four kinds of wood were used to assemble the ladder. With the national media reporting on the trial, the world listened in stunned amazement as Koehler identified each of these four types. He was also able to determine, using a microscope, that the wood used to make the ladder was purchased from a lumber yard less than 10 miles (16 kilometers) from the defendant's home. Hauptmann was found guilty and later sentenced to death for the kidnapping and death of the Lindbergh baby.

Forensic botany is still not a well-known field, but botanists are oftentimes called on to testify in cases where plant evidence may prove essential to solving a crime. Oftentimes, criminals and their victims carry with them evidence of where they have been in the form of plant materials. These seeds, pollen, and plant fibers can ultimately lead to conviction of the guilty party.

tube elements are largely hollow cells that form in long chains within a plant. They contain holes to allow the sugars made through photosynthesis to move throughout the plant. Companion cells are not hollow and act as support structures for the sieve tube elements.

SPECIALIZED CELLS IN THE ROOT, STEM, AND LEAVES

When looking at a plant, we must realize that we are seeing only a portion of that living organism. In some cases, the majority of the plant's mass actually grows underground. Much of the activity in plants occurs under the surface where root systems are spreading out into the soil, serving to stabilize the plant and to anchor it so it will not be easily blown away by the wind or pulled out of the ground by herbivores. Roots also absorb nutrients like nitrogen, phosphorus, and potassium as well as water from the soil to supply these nutrients to the rest of the plant.

The essential role of roots in the life of a plant would not be possible were it not for highly specialized plant cells that go to work immediately after a new plant germinates. For the seedling to survive, the root system must quickly anchor the young plant and begin drawing in water so that the process of photosynthesis can begin.

The first task that the root of a newly germinated seedling must complete is to anchor itself in the ground. (This is not always easy because the seed may have fallen on hard, rocky soil that it cannot penetrate.) Roots have highly specialized epidermal cells that are very thick and tough called root caps. Root caps quickly work their way through the soil, insuring that the seedling will be stable in even the worst ground. The caps have the unique ability to use the force of gravity to insure that they grow straight downward. To aid them in implanting in hard soil, they release a slimy secretion called mucilage that acts to lubricate the plant as it grows deeper into the soil.

Another type of specialized cell in the epidermis of the root helps to form root hairs. Root hairs grow out into the soil surrounding the root and act like sponges, drawing in water through osmosis. This water is then transferred to the xylem to be carried throughout the plant.

The bulk of the roots' cells lie just under the epidermis. Most of these cells are ground tissue that is classified in three groups. The first group of ground tissue lies closest to the tip of the root and is known as the **zone of cell division**. In this zone, cells are rapidly going through the process of mitosis. Their continued growth pushes the root cap even deeper into the soil. The leading edge of the zone of division closest to the root cap is known as the **apical meristem**. The apical meristem is where the fastest reproduction occurs and where the youngest cells can be found.

Beside the zone of cell division lies the second group of ground tissue, the **zone of elongation**. The zone of elongation is the region of the root where cells begin to fill with water and turgor pressure causes them to expand. This increase in pressure within the root assists the root cap as it works its way through the soil.

Just above the zone of elongation lies the third group of ground tissue, the **zone of maturation**. The zone of maturation is where plant cells in the root begin to differentiate. This is also the portion of the root where most of the water enters the plant because the root hairs grow out from the epidermis in this region.

The stem of the plant also has an apical meristem. This is the tallest portion of the plant or tree where cells are rapidly reproducing and growing. The growth of a plant up and down from the apical meristems is known as **primary growth**. However, plants not only grow straight up and down, but also grow outward, expanding the reach of their roots and their limbs as they mature. Growth that does not occur from the apical meristems is known as **secondary growth**.

If a plant continued to grow taller and taller, year after year, without getting any thicker, what would happen to that plant? The answer is that sooner or later, the weight of the apical meristem would be too much and the plant would collapse. Because of this, plants must undergo secondary growth that thickens the stems, limbs, and trunk so that the weight of the growing plant can be supported.

During secondary growth, cell growth occurs in two primary regions: The first region is the vascular cambium. The vascular cambium is where vascular tissue is produced. This is the innermost region of secondary growth in plant cells. The vascular cambium continues producing more cells as it expands outward. As new vascular tissue in plants is formed, older vascular tissue is no longer used and it stops working. Over time, as the new vascular cambium continues its outward growth, the nonfunctional cambium from years past ceases carrying water and becomes inactive. This accounts for the rings that can be seen in trees that mark periods of growth.

Cork cambium, the second region for primary growth, produces the outermost layer of the stem in plants and, along with the vascular cambium, is responsible for secondary growth in the plant. The cork cambium continues to grow and expand, forming a protective shield of oils that protect and waterproof the tree. As the cork cambium expands, it produces a strong outer layer that protects the plant. In trees we recognize this as bark.

The cells in the stems of some plant species are highly specialized to perform specific tasks. Potatoes, for instance, grow special food storage compartments from their stems that are called **tubers**. You may have seen a bag of potatoes that appear to have sprouted roots while still in the bag. These are tubers, and although they appear like roots they are actually portions of the plant stem that are dedicated to storing food. **Rhizomes** are portions of a plant stem that grow along the surface of the ground, or just below it. These portions can grow to form new plants. As a result, what appears to be several different plants may all belong to one set of roots. As rhizomes spread out they can sprout new leaves in areas far away from the root of the plant. Thick mats of rhizomes can sometimes be located just below the surface of the ground.

FIGURE 7.4 Strawberry plants are connected by rhizomes that grow along the surface of the ground.

Leaves contain many specialized cells that help with gas exchange and the process of photosynthesis. Among the most specialized cells in plants are **guard cells** that protect the plant from water loss. Guard cells form openings called stomata on the underside of the plant. As previously discussed, gases are required for the photosynthetic process, and they must travel through the stomata. Guard cells have the ability to open and close stomata like a mouth, which can increase the rate of gas exchange, slow it down or sometimes even completely shut it off to prevent water loss. This last action occurs most often during the hottest months of the summer.

Some species of plants grow in very harsh conditions. Other species grow in areas where there is a great deal of competition for space and light. In order to compete, some plants have developed highly specialized cells and tissues that provide them with an advantage in these harsh climates.

Plants cannot defend themselves by running away, so they must have defenses that protect them as they grow in one location. One form of defense is toxins. **Toxins** are chemicals that the plant's cells produce to

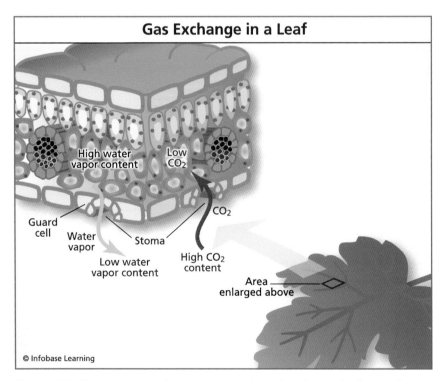

FIGURE 7.5 The exchange of oxygen and carbon dioxide in a leaf, as well as the loss of water vapor during transpiration, occurs through pores called stomata.

protect it from predators. Some of these toxins are deadly to insects, while others are fatal to mammals and, in some cases, even humans. The Greek philosopher Socrates, for example, died when he was forced to ingest the poisonous roots of the hemlock plant. Cells in oak trees produce toxins known as tannins that repel insects. The seeds of some plants, like the deadly jimson weed, can cause hallucinations and death in humans. Plant cells serve as the factory where these toxins are developed.

Plants in very dry environments have specialized cells designed to conserve water and maintain photosynthesis in some of the world's harshest deserts. Plants that have special defenses against the dryness and the heat of the desert are known as **xerophytes.** All xerophytes have specially developed cells that overcome many obstacles—hot temperatures, poor soil, little rain, and drastic changes in temperature. Xerophytes have developed a variety of ways to cope with the difficulties of living in the desert, including the ability to store large amounts of water in specialized cells within the plant (this is why cacti and other xerophytes are sometimes referred to as succulents, or plants with thick, water-filled leaves and stems). Because xerophytes have spines instead of leaves, little or no water is lost through the stomata. They also have specialized roots that spread out widely across the ground, creating a network of small, thin hairs that absorb rainwater before it sinks into the sandy desert soil.

There are very few plants that can survive in the extreme conditions of the desert. However, some plants have too many neighbors. Rainforests, for example, are home to many plants that are constantly in competition for a limited amount of resources. Sunlight is one of these resources. Many plants that live in the rain forest die because they do not receive enough sunlight to undergo photosynthesis. However, some plants do not need to grow on the ground. In fact, one of their favorite places to grow is on other plants. These "hitchhiker" plants are known as **epiphytes**. By germinating and growing on other plants high up in the canopy of the rainforest, epiphytes have an opportunity to receive sunlight that many similarly sized plants growing down on the forest floor do not have. This adaptation allows epiphytes to outcompete other plants. Epiphytic plants often have very specialized cells that perform tasks like water collection. Most plants pull water from the ground through their roots, but epiphytes do not have this ability. Epiphytes, therefore, must have specialized tissues that can collect water to keep the plant hydrated.

It may seem as though epiphytes would damage their host plant. A few of them, like the strangler fig, are, indeed, harmful to the plant they live on. Strangler figs send down roots that dig into the soil and, eventually, the

FIGURE 7.6 Saguaro cacti, pictured in Arizona, can hold in about 200 gallons (757 liters) of water and make it last for a year.

strangler fig overwhelms and kills the host plant. However, most epiphytes cause little or no damage to their hosts. They have specialized cells in their roots that act as anchors to hold them to other plants. Most orchids, for example, are epiphytes, growing high in the rain forest canopy away from the shade and predators on the forest floor. Spanish moss, which hangs from other trees like a series of green curtains, is another example of an epiphyte.

Some plants have even adapted methods of capturing prey to supplement their diet of the sugar produced by photosynthesis. These are known as carnivorous plants, the most famous of which is the Venus flytrap. Flytraps, like the vast majority of carnivorous plants, grow in places where the soil is not rich enough to provide the nutrients required by the plant. To combat this, carnivorous plants supplement their sugary diet with nutrients from the insects they capture. Venus flytraps have special sensory cells that are located between two modified leaves. These cells form tissues that are touch sensitive. They close when they are touched by the legs of insects that have mistaken the flytrap's jaws for a flower. When the touch-sensitive portion of the plant responds to the insect's presence, the leaves shut like a mouth, trapping the insect inside.

Flytraps, however, are not the only carnivorous plant. Pitcher plants also have the ability to break down insects that become trapped inside them. The stem of the plant is roughly the shape of a vase or pitcher (hence the name) and when insects enter, expecting a meal of pollen, they fall into a cocktail of enzymes that are secreted by specialized cells in the plant's stem. As the insect begins to break down in the enzyme juice, its nutrients are absorbed by other specialized cells in the plant.

With the exception of the extreme polar regions of the Earth, plants have managed to survive in almost every imaginable condition and locale. In the hottest deserts and on high mountain peaks, plants have beaten the odds and found a way to survive despite harsh conditions. Much of the success of these plants is due to the highly specialized cells that give them the ability to overcome extreme challenges.

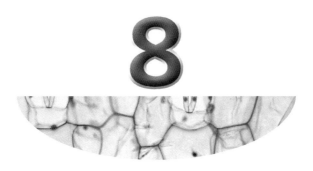

8

Biotechnology

In the hills of central Tennessee, not far from the city of Knoxville, a series of brick buildings sprawl across a wooded hill. This facility is known as Oak Ridge National Laboratory, and it is home to some of the most advanced research facilities in the world. Originally built during the 1940s to house researchers working on the Manhattan Project, Oak Ridge now has more than 4,600 scientists who work to solve some of the world's most puzzling questions and provide solutions to serious problems like global food shortages and our dependence on fossil fuels. Here, highly trained scientists work with the most state-of-the-art equipment to unlock the energy hidden within one of the world's most sophisticated organisms: plants.

The scientists at Oak Ridge understand that plants may help us to cure diseases, provide food for starving nations, and reduce or even eliminate our dependence on nonrenewable energy sources like coal and oil. The U.S. Department of Energy has backed a variety of research topics at Oak Ridge that involve plants and their potential to change the world.

As you have learned, plant cells are complex units that have superbly adapted to survive in a variety of conditions. Plants can be a source of energy that does not create damaging byproducts. Their cells store large amounts of energy that can provide the fuel we need to feed our bodies, run our cars, and power electric plants. Scientists are only beginning to discover new potential uses for plants. One thing is also certain—plants and plant cell technology are essential to our future in regard to energy

FIGURE 8.1 A scientist at Oak Ridge National Laboratory examines bacteria isolated from a poplar tree rhizosphere. Scientists at the lab study interactions between microbes and plants in order to gain a basic understanding of how they use chemical signals to communicate.

consumption, now that we are recognizing the need to find alternative resources to fulfill the needs of a rapidly growing global human population.

There are a variety of projects going on at Oak Ridge and other facilities around the country that center on the potential benefits that plants offer us.

GMOs AND GEOs

One of the most controversial topics in science today revolves around the safety and value of **genetically modified organisms (GMOs)**, which contain genes that have been manipulated and altered for some purpose. To modify genes in a plant, scientists must first find the location of the gene they wish to alter in the plant's genome. Mapping genomes involves identifying which locations on which chromosomes contain genetic

... UNWELCOME VISITORS ...

One of the biggest threats to wildlife is the introduction of plant and animal species that are not native to an area. These transplanted organisms, known as invasive species, can seriously harm the ecosystems into which they are introduced and cost millions of dollars annually to control. Oftentimes, the people responsible for the introduction of these alien species have no idea what they are doing. In fact, many invasive plants are introduced by people who simply want to plant gardens of beautiful, exotic plants around their homes. Sometimes, though, these plants spread and compete with local plants, forever altering the native ecosystem.

One example of an invasive plant is kudzu, an Asian vine that spreads very quickly and takes over land once occupied by native plants, oftentimes killing these plants in the process. Kudzu was originally introduced into the United States to help control erosion. Soon, however, the vine began to grow out of control to cover trees, hillsides, abandoned cars, and even buildings. In the southeastern United States, millions of dollars are spent annually in the fight against kudzu.

Another invasive plant is Russian olive, a thorny shrub that was introduced to the United States in the late nineteenth century as an ornamental plant. Russian olive soon spread into rural areas and began outcompeting native plants, reducing the food supply for herbivores and

information that codes for a certain trait, such as resistance to drought or indirect sunlight. Through a process called genome sequencing, scientists at Oak Ridge and at other facilities across the country have learned to identify the genomic locations of a variety of important plant traits. The desired genes are inserted into the genome at the proper location. Sometimes, these genes come from other organisms, such as bacteria that have a desired trait such as resistance to specific chemicals. When the gene is placed at the proper location, the host plant carries that particular characteristic throughout its life. Organisms that have been genetically manipulated in this way are also sometimes referred to as **genetically engineered organisms (GEOs)**.

leaving the native habitat unbalanced and reducing or even eliminating native species of plants and animals.

It is important that invasive species be identified and controlled. Avoid planting nonnative ornamentals near your house to help reduce the impact of invasive species near you.

Figure 8.2 Kudzu, particularly common in the southeastern United States, covers most of a home in this image.

According to the Oak Ridge National Laboratory, as of 2007, there were more than 250 million acres (101 million hectares) of GMO crops planted around the world. Genetically modified plants contain DNA that allows them to grow more quickly, resist drought, produce natural insecticides, and to be tolerant of herbicides that farmers spray on crops to kill weeds. Some GMO plants have the ability to produce more fruit and allow farmers in poor regions of the world like sub-Saharan Africa to increase the yield of their crops and so increase the food supply in poor rural areas. Some GMOs even taste better than traditional crops of the same species.

GMO plants can provide other products for consumers besides food. Certain plants can be modified to produce medicines for use in the fight

FIGURE 8.3 Two cultivated potato plants are pictured. The plant on the left has not been not genetically modified, but the plant on the right has been modified to be resistant against *Phytophthora infestans*, which is believed to be what caused the Irish potato famine in the 1840s.

against diseases like hepatitis and cancer. Plants can also be modified to produce materials for use in the production of plastic goods and clothing. New varieties of flowering plants can be produced to add color and variety to gardens. These plants can also produce their own natural insecticides.

The technology that produced GMOs has not been accepted by all scientists, though. Despite the many benefits of GMOs, there are still some concerns about the impact that genetically modified foods like corn and rice may have on consumers. Increases in food supplies are good for countries where food shortages occur regularly, but the long term effects of a diet high in GMOs is still uncertain. In many areas, GMO plants are required to be planted far enough away from non-GMO plants so that cross-pollination between GMOs and non-GMO plants is unlikely to occur. There is also concern that biotechnology companies will have the ability to provide or withhold GMOs to certain areas or countries, and that this power could be manipulated by political or industrial powers. Labeling GMOs may also prove to be a problem. Some groups want all GMOs to be plainly labeled so that consumers will know that they are purchasing food that has been genetically modified, and they believe consumers should be aware that the long-term effects of GMOs are not well understood or researched.

Manipulating the DNA of plants has allowed scientists to discover possible solutions to the problems of increasing human populations and less space for farmlands as urban areas spread out onto land that was once

OAK RIDGE NATIONAL LABORATORY

Oak Ridge National Laboratory in Tennessee is working hard to develop new methods of energy to reduce pollution and the world's reliance on fossil fuels. Plants will likely play a large role in this project. So far, biomass is proving to be one of the most promising sources of clean, renewable energy available today. Nevertheless, plant fuels are just one of the areas that Oak Ridge scientists are now exploring.

Computers have changed the way that scientists conduct their research. Each year, computer technology brings about new advances that help scientists solve problems that once seemed impossible to remedy. Few research laboratories, however, have computers that can compete with the one located at Oak Ridge's Center for Computational Sciences. This massive computer has the ability to conduct 1,600 trillion calculations per second. In addition, Oak Ridge is also working on improving materials sciences and developing new materials to replace existing plastics and metals. The lab is also working to solve some of the country's most pressing issues, including improving the existing power grid, providing clean-burning fuels from renewable materials, and making solar power more available and affordable. In addition to these ambitious goals, the lab is also working to decrease the threat of terrorism with new technologies that can alert the government to potential threats.

Many of the world's best scientists work at Oak Ridge, which employs over 4,000 scientists from 80 different countries. With the lab's ambitious projects and their $1.4 billion budget, working at Oak Ridge is a dream for many aspiring scientists.

used for farming. However, the question remains whether or not GMOs will provide an answer to these challenges.

BIOMASS

One of the most pressing problems that we face in the twenty-first century is how to reduce the world's reliance on fossil fuel energy sources. Fossil fuels like gasoline and petroleum-based diesel fuels are nonrenewable resources, and there are varying estimates regarding the amount of oil that remains on Earth. In addition, burning fossil fuels in cars, homes, and businesses creates pollution and adds high levels of carbon dioxide into the air. Carbon dioxide is believed to be a major factor in global warming.

Scientists are working hard to find an alternative energy source that will replace fossil fuels, decrease our demand on oil, and protect the environment. One of the most promising sources of alternative fuel is biomass. Biomass fuel sources typically come from crops. These crops are known as biomass energy crops. According to Oak Ridge National Laboratory, biomass energy crops "are trees and perennial grasses grown specifically to provide raw materials (also known as feedstock) for energy producers and industry." The energy stores that are locked in plant cells can be burned, and the energy in the bonds within plant cells operate everything from cars to conveyor belts in factories.

The U.S. Department of Energy is currently researching which raw plant materials seem to be the most effective for producing biomass that can be easily converted to biomass energy. One plant that appears to have the most potential as an energy source as biomass is switchgrass. Switchgrass is a monocot grass native to the American prairies. It once provided food for birds and mammal species and prevented devastating erosion on the plains. As European settlers moved west, much of the switchgrass prairie was wiped out and replaced by agricultural land. Tilling of the land and the introduction of nonnative plants increased soil erosion on the plains and destroyed the food supply for many native species. As the demand for biomass materials increases, farmers on the plains are seeing the value in planting switchgrass. In addition to its value as a biomass material, switchgrass will also provide food and cover for native animals as well as preventing the large-scale erosion that has been caused by traditional methods of tilling for food crops. In addition to using crops specifically planted and harvested for biomass, Oak Ridge laboratory is also exploring ways for using recycled paper products and wood from

FIGURE 8.4 Switchgrass is pictured on a prairie. In part because it is native to North America, switchgrass is resistant to many pests and plant diseases. It is also capable of producing high yields with very little fertilizer.

demolished structures as additional sources of biomass energy. This will help reduce waste in landfills while producing energy.

One of the major concerns facing the environment is the emission of carbon dioxide gas from the burning of fossil fuels. Scientists are currently testing the effectiveness of plant-based alternative vehicle fuels like biodiesel, which is an alternative to traditional petroleum-based diesel that is used in the engines of many passenger vehicles and large trucks. Biodiesel is derived from vegetable oils, which can be used to power a vehicle. In addition to reducing dependence on fossil fuels, biodiesel also produces fewer emissions than traditional fuel sources like gasoline and petroleum-based diesel fuel.

PLANTS AS MEDICINES

Long before modern medicine offered the synthetic pharmaceutical drugs that we take today, early doctors relied heavily on the chemical compounds found in plants to help alleviate and cure many diseases. Humans around the world have relied on the healing powers of medicinal plants to help with medical problems ranging from cramps to cancer. Today, pharmaceutical

HOW TO GET INVOLVED

Anyone can help save rare plants around the world. Here's how to get involved:

- Many of the world's most important medicinal plants are found in the rainforest—and many of these species have the potential to cure diseases like cancer. Some of them have not yet even been discovered. One group working to prevent the loss of rare plants in the rainforest is the Nature Conservancy (www.nature.org), a worldwide leader in preservation.
- Educate your friends, neighbors, and community about the dangers of invasive species: Even though it may seem harmless to spread nonnative plants to new habitats, the results can be devastating. Nonnative plants can drive out native species and disrupt an entire ecosystem. The first step to stopping the spread of invasive species is by spreading the word about the dangers they pose. Visit www.invasivespeciesinfo.gov.
- Reduce waste and help improve the soil. Compost piles are an effective way to turn waste like banana peels and other food waste into topsoil and fertilizer. However, before you compost, be sure that you know how to do it so that you can have a positive impact.
- Plant a tree. Today, one of the most pressing concerns facing environmentalists is global warming. You can help reduce carbon dioxide levels in the air by simply planting a tree. It is fun, easy and will leave a lasting legacy behind for years to come. For more information visit www.arborday.org.
- Visit the center of the most current research on biomass fuels: Oak Ridge National Laboratory (www.ornl.gov) near Knoxville, Tennessee, is conducting groundbreaking research on alternative fuel sources to reduce our dependence on oil. Oak Ridge is home to over 4,000 of the world's best scientists and you can visit the facilities where they work.

companies are researching the chemicals in plants, hoping to find possible cures for some of the most deadly diseases.

The history of medicinal plants predates written records. The healing power of willow leaves was first recorded by Hippocrates of Cos almost 2,500 years ago. Hippocrates wrote that chewing on willow leaves and bark helped alleviate a variety of painful conditions, everything from head-aches to childbirth. Hippocrates was the first person on record to note the healing power of the chemical salicylic acid. Willow leaves contain high levels of this natural painkiller, the formula for which would later become the basis for the drug we know as aspirin.

Not all plant remedies worked as well as willow leaves, though. Doc-tors with varying levels of training prescribed plant medicines and offered healing herbs. Many of these herbs had little or no effect on the conditions they were prescribed to cure. Some plants, however, haven proven particu-larly useful to people across generations. In South America, for instance, the medicinal uses of coca leaves as stimulants and painkillers have long been known and documented. Another South American plant, cinchona, was originally used as a pain killer and to relieve tremors. It was later also discovered that one of the chemicals found in cinchona, called quinine, could prevent and alleviate the symptoms of malaria, an infectious disease that is spread by mosquitoes. The use of quinine from cinchona plants during a 1631 malaria epidemic in Rome saved thousands of victims from long, painful deaths.

Today, pharmaceutical companies are investigating the potential ben-efits of chemical compounds found naturally in wild plants. Bloodroot, for instance, contains chemicals that have proven effective at shrinking tumors in some cancer patients. The Oregon grape, a plant harvested in the Pacific Northwest, has the potential to help alleviate discomfort from skin conditions and may also have antibiotic properties.

Pharmaceutical researchers are not the only ones taking note of the healing potential of plant chemicals. Officials at the U.S. National Park Service estimate that more than 60 million Americans use plants and plants derivatives to help cure or prevent diseases.

From fertilization to germination and beyond, plants are miracles of evolution. They have the ability to produce their own food, reproduce without moving, and lie dormant during periods of stress. Plants can sur-vive fires, droughts, and bitter cold temperatures thanks to their highly specialized cellular processes. In addition, plants cloth us, provide us with food and shelter, and even heal us when we are sick. Plants are some of smallest living organisms, and they are the largest and oldest, as well. They come in an endless variety of shapes and sizes that thrive in every environment except the polar regions. From the common to the extreme, from the tiny mosses that live on the forest floor to towering redwood trees that seem to reach into the heavens, all plants, no matter how big or small, began as a single cell.

Glossary

adenosine triphosphate (ATP)   The source of cellular energy

alternation of generations   Cycle of diploid and haploid stages in plant lifecycle

anaphase   Third stage in mitosis and meiosis characterized by the separation of cellular material toward opposite poles

anemochoric   Plants that are pollinated by the wind

angiosperms   Flowering plants

anthers   Filaments that contain pollen

apical meristem   Leading edge of the zone of division closest to the root cap

apoptosis   Prescribed cell death

autotroph   Organism capable of producing its own food

biology   Study of living organisms

capillary action   Movement of water upward in a tube because of the cohesive, or self-bonding properties of water

cell membrane   Separates cell wall from interior of cell

cell theory   States that all living things are made of cells, that cells create more cells, and that cells are the building blocks of living organisms.

cellular lysis   Cell bursting or splitting

cellular respiration   The process of converting light energy to chemical energy through photosynthesis

cell wall   Outermost portion of the plant cell characterized by stiff borders made of cellulose

chlorophyll   Green pigment found in the chloroplasts of plants; it is necessary for photosynthesis.

chloroplasts   Organelles that contain chlorophyll and act as the site of photosynthesis

chromatids   Bundles of chromosomes

chromatin   Tightly coiled chromosomes in the nucleus of a cell

chromoplast   Plastids inside the plant cell that are responsible for pigment storage

chromosomes   Tightly coiled strands of DNA

collenchyma   Ground tissue cells that are flexible and have thickened cell walls capable of withstanding large amounts of strain

companion cells   Act as support structures for the sieve tube elements

cristae   Folds within the mitochondria

cuticle   Waxy layer on top of the epidermis

cystol   Fluid matrix within the cell that is not enclosed within organelle membranes

daughter cells   Identical copies of genetic information that begin to separate during anaphase

deoxyribonucleic acid (DNA)   Nucleic acid that contains genetic information used in the development and functioning of living organisms

dermal plant tissues   Protects the plant from the outside environment

desiccation   Drying out

dicotyledons   Group of plants characterized by seeds with two cotyledons

dioecious   Species of plants that have separate male and female plants

electron transport chain   Release of energy during light reactions of photosynthesis

endosperm   Carbohydrates that provide nutrition to growing embryo

endosymbiosis   One organism living within another organism and functioning as a single organism

epiphytes   Plants that grow on other plants

eukaryotes   Cells that contain a well-defined nucleus with a nuclear membrane

fruit   Thickened walls of ovaries that contain fertilized seeds

gametophyte   Haploid (n) phase of the plant life cycle

genes   Inherited genetic material

GEO/GMO   Genetically engineered organism or genetically modified organism; an organism containing DNA that has been added or modified by scientists in an effort to produce qualities in the organism that do not occur naturally

germination   Process in which the embryonic plant bursts through the seed coat and begins the process of independent food production

Golgi apparatus   Organelle responsible for the packaging and shipment of materials within and out of the cell

grana   Stacks of membranes inside the chloroplasts

ground tissue   Cells that lie between the dermal tissue and the inner vascular tissue in plants

guard cells   Specialized cells that protect the plant from water loss

gymnosperms   Cone-bearing plants, literally "naked seed"

heredity   The study of genetic inheritance

homologous pairs   Identical pairs of chromosomes

hybrid   The result of cross-pollination between very closely related species

hypertonic solution   Solution where there is more salt outside the cell than inside

hypotonic solution   Solution where there is more salt inside the cell than outside

inorganic materials   Molecules that do not contain carbon

interphase   Phase in cells just before meiosis and mitosis begin

macromolecules   Large, highly specialized molecules

mesophyll   Interior portion of the leaf

metaphase   Second stage of meiosis and mitosis characterized by chromosomes aligned along center line of the cell

mitochondria   Organelle that provides energy for the cell

mitosis   Process of cell division for the purpose of growth and cellular regeneration

monocotyledons   Group of plants characterized by seeds containing a single cotyledon

monoecious   Single plants with both male and female reproductive parts

nuclear lamina   Gives structure to the nucleus and helps it maintain its shape

nucleus   Organelle in a cell that contains genetic material that codes for protein synthesis

organelle   The organs of a cell

organs   Collection of tissues that serve a specific function in the life of the organism

ovary   Contains the ovule

ovule   Female reproductive cell of the plant

parenchyma   Thin-walled cells with large openings within each cell

pH   Measure of how acidic or basic a substance is; ranges from 0–14, with 7 being neutral

phloem   Collection of highly specialized cells, called sieve tube elements, and companion cells that form tubes dedicated to the transport of nutrients within the plant

photons   Units of light energy

photosynthesis   Process of creating food from light energy

pistil   Female portion of the flower containing the stigma, style, and ovary

plasmodesmata   Channels in cell walls

pollinator   An organism that fertilizes plants by carrying pollen from one plant to another

prickles   Extensions of the plant that are developed to protect that plant and that have a sharp point like those found on flowers like roses

primary growth   Growth of a plant up and down from the apical meristems

prokaryotes   Cells that lack a nuclear membrane

prophase   First stage of mitosis and meiosis characterized by darkening chromosomes

radicle   Initial root of an immature plant

rhizomes   Portions of a plant stem that grow along the surface of the ground or just below it and can form other plants

ribosomes   Organelles responsible for protein production

sclerenchyma   Ground tissue cells that have little fluid inside of them and have very rigid cell walls that provide the plant cell with support

secondary growth Growth that does not occur from the apical meristems

seeds Structures designed to protect the developing plant embryo

selectively permeable membrane Membrane that only allows certain items to pass through

semipermeable membrane See **selectively permeable membrane**

sieve tube elements Largely hollow cells that form in long chains within a plant; they have holes in them to allow sugars made through photosynthesis to be moved throughout the plant.

sori Plant spores found on ferns and related plants

spines Modified leaves that protect the plant like those found on cacti

sporophyte Diploid ($2n$) stage of the plant life cycle

stamen Male portion of the flower

stigma Superior (uppermost) portion of the pistil

stomata Openings in leaves for gas exchange

style Tube that carries pollen to the ovule

taproot Large, single root that is characteristic of dicotyledon plants

telophase The final stage in mitosis and meiosis

thorns Modified portions of the plant stem designed for defense of the plant

thylakoids (or thylakoid membranes) Location of light-dependent reactions of photosynthesis in the chloroplast

tissues Groups of cells with a similar structure

toxins Chemicals that plants use for defense

transpiration Water lost through evaporation

tubers Special food storage compartments in the stems of some plants

vacuole Organelle within the cell that is surrounded by a membrane and contains a liquid solution of water and other materials such as enzymes

vascular tissue Plant tissue that contains xylem and phloem

visible spectrum Wavelengths of light visible to the human eye

xerophytes Plants that have special defenses against the dryness and the heat of the desert

xylem   Plant tissue that transports water through a series of specialized cells called tracheids

zone of cell division   Ground tissue closest to the tip of the root

zone of elongation   Region of the root where cells begin to fill with water; turgor pressure causes the cells to expand.

zone of maturation   Area where plant cells in the root begin to differentiate

zoochoric   Plants that are pollinated by animals

zygote   Plant embryo

Bibliography

"Bioenergy Science Program" *Research Advancing the Bioenergy Supply Chain.* Oak Ridge National Laboratory. June 2009. Available online at http://www.ornl.gov/sci/bioenergy/. Accessed October 30, 2010.

Biondo, Ronald J. *Greenhouse Production.* Upper Saddle River, N.J.: Pearson Education, Inc., 2004.

Daniel, Lucy, Ed Ortleb, and Alton Biggs. *Life Science.* New York: Glencoe/McGraw-Hill, 1999.

Lindsay, Mary, ed. *The Visual Dictionary of Plants.* New York: Dorling Kindersley, Inc., 1992.

Miller, Kenneth R. and Joseph S. Levine. *Biology.* Upper Saddle River, N.J.: Pearson Education, Inc., 2004.

Wayne, Randy. *Plant Cell Biology.* Burlington, Mass.: Elsevier, 2009.

Yatskievych, Kay. *Field Guide to Indiana Wildflowers.* Bloomington, Ind.: Indiana University Press, 2000.

Video

Plant. DK Eyewitness Video. 1997.

Further Resources

Books

Hewitt, Sally. *Fascinating Science Projects: Plants*. Brookfield, Conn.: Copper Beech Books, 2001.

Raven, Peter H. *Biology of Plants*. New York: W.H. Freeman, 2004.

Smith, Allison M., George Coupland, Liam Dolan, Nicholas Harberd et al. *Plant Biology*. London: Garland Science, 2009.

Taylor, Charles, ed. *The Kingfisher Science Encyclopedia*. New York: Kingfisher Publishing, 2000.

Web Sites

Arbor Day Foundation
www.arborday.org
This nonprofit organization promotes planting trees and encourages people to become more involved in issues regarding America's forests.

Botanical Society of America
www.botany.org
Find more information about forensic botany.

Lady Bird Johnson Wildflower Center at The University of Texas at Austin
http://www.wildflower.org/explore/
Claudia Alta "Lady Bird" Johnson, the late wife of former president Lyndon B. Johnson, loved plants her entire life. Now the Lady Bird Johnson Wildflower Center promotes the conservation of native wildflowers.

The Nature Conservancy
www.nature.org.
The conservancy is a worldwide leader in preservation. This member-supported organization has helped to protect areas of ecological importance in all 50 States and 30 foreign countries.

Nobelprize.org
http://nobelprize.org/
This is the official site of the Nobel Prize Committee. The Nobel Prize is named in honor of Alfred Nobel, a Swedish scientist, author, and pacifist who

left his fortune for the establishment of the prize. The award is given annually to outstanding individual accomplishments in the fields of chemistry, physics, medicine, literature and peace.

Oak Ridge National Laboratory Bioenergy
http://www.ornl.gov/sci/bioenergy/

Oak Ridge National Laboratory is facing one of the nation's greatest challenges: reducing our reliance on oil. Plants may play a large role in producing renewable energy. The laboratory has programs for visitors.

UBC Botanical Garden and Centre for Plant Research
http://www.ubcbotanicalgarden.org/

UBC Botanical Garden in British Columbia, Canada, maintains a variety of gardens containing native and non-native plants. It is also one of the largest databases for plant information.

USDA Plant Database
http://plants.usda.gov/

The U.S. Department of Agriculture maintains a variety of informative pages on invasive plants, prairie grasses, and threats to native plants, such as borer beetles.

Picture Credits

page:

Index

About the Author

Brad Fitzpatrick earned his bachelor's degree in biological science from Northern Kentucky University in Highland Heights, Kentucky. He has written for over twenty different magazines, including *Sports Afield, Cincinnati, Over the Back Fence,* and *American Cowboy*. Brad conducted research on mosquitoes in Costa Rica's Osa Peninsula and has studied cheetahs in Namibia. He currently teaches biotechnology at Southern Hills Career Center in Georgetown, Ohio.